'*Donkey Roads and Camel Tre[...]al
journey through Advent. Gem[...]h
gentleness and challenge in [...]is
us with tenderness and leads us into transformation.'
The Revd Preb Dr Isabelle Hamley, principal of Ridley Hall,
Cambridge and author of *Embracing Humanity*

'Advent is a time of great anticipation, and as Gemma says in her charming, inspiring and frequently profound new book, one of her favourite times of year. But what happens when all our plans for a spiritual Advent, filled with deep prayer and peaceful meditation, run into the reality of our often complicated and complex lives? In these beautifully written and artfully presented meditations, Gemma reminds us that the first Christmas also took place in a complicated and complex world, and that God is ready to accompany us in our messy lives, whether we're in a car, at our desk, in our living room or, yes, atop a camel.'
James Martin, SJ, author of *Learning to Pray*

'An attractive and inspiring travel invitation. I immediately wanted to get a special journal to walk with the reflections through Advent. The questions at the end of each section are real gems – places to pause to consider the invitations hidden in the reflections. Indeed, the journey might even be richer if shared with a group of friends.'
Bernadette Flanagan, spiritual director and co-founder
of The Spirituality Institute for Research and Education

'Whether you want to find fresh ways to connect with God, with each other, with nature or with your own deepest desires, this book will inspire you. I do not know a wiser spiritual guide to ordinary Christian living than Gemma Simmonds. Here, from her life of immersion in prayer, wisdom-seeking, formation of individuals and communities, and practical service in some extremely demanding situations, she offers a deeply attractive distillation, focused through key biblical texts. This is far more than an imaginative, thoughtful and practical way to approach Christmas; it gives the essentials for a lifetime following Jesus.'
David F. Ford OBE, Regius professor of divinity emeritus,
Selwyn College, University of Cambridge

 Ministries

15 The Chambers, Vineyard
Abingdon OX14 3FE
+44 (0)1865 319700 | brf.org.uk

Bible Reading Fellowship (BRF) is a charity (233280)
and company limited by guarantee (301324),
registered in England and Wales

EU Authorised Representative: Easy Access System Europe – Mustamäe tee 50,
10621 Tallinn, Estonia, **gpsr.requests@easproject.com**

ISBN 978 1 80039 347 9
First published 2025
10 9 8 7 6 5 4 3 2 1 0
All rights reserved

A catalogue record for this book is available from the British Library

Printed by CPI Group (UK) Ltd, Croydon CR0 4YY

DONKEY ROADS AND CAMEL TREKS

A pilgrim's guide
for Advent

Gemma Simmonds

BRF
Ministries

To my wonderful brother-in-law, Anthony Gibbons, a resolute and understatedly faithful Anglican amid a gaggle of off-the-wall Catholic in-laws, who died just before Advent 2023. He would have been the best companion to come along with me on a donkey road or a camel trek. Travel disasters would have been calmly overcome, inns booked far in advance, animals cared for meticulously and food and drink relished, whatever their provenance. His Advent is over, the dawn has come and his God is truly with him now.

Contents

WEEK 3 HOPE IN DARKNESS

WEEK 4 TRANSFORMATION

Acknowledgements

I always approach writing, especially spiritual writing, with a mixture of excitement, reluctance and terror.

The excitement is because writing is a way of working out what I actually think, deep down, when I take sufficient time to look, and of understanding what God is up to in the world and within those who share their faith, doubt and searching questions with me.

The reluctance is partly because it awakens a level of imposter syndrome in me – why would anyone want to spend time and hard-earned money reading what I have got to say – and what have I got to say on this particular subject that is remotely new or interesting?

Writing inspires terror because, unlike Douglas Adams, I don't love the whooshing noise that deadlines make as they go by.

But if I can summon up the courage to get going, then I couldn't be in better hands than those of BRF Ministries, who take encouragement to a whole new level. So, thank you to Olivia Warburton, Felicity Howlett and Rachel Tranter, who, in their different capacities, have been immeasurably patient and kind, as well as superbly professional. You and BRF Ministries have done me great honour by inviting me to write these reflections.

And thank you to my colleagues past and present on the BBC Daily Service, especially Philip Billson and Claire Jaquiss, whose comments and consummate skill as communicators over the years have taught me so much about trying to speak of spiritual matters in accessible terms.

Finally, thank you to Sister Mary Richard Prendergast and the late Sister Francis North of the Congregation of Jesus, two consummate teachers who, at primary and secondary school level, taught me to love the written, read and spoken word in English and Latin and guided me through innumerable nativity plays, Christmas carols and Advent reflections to my huge enjoyment.

Introduction

I tend to approach Advent with mixed feelings. It is my favourite liturgical season, and I usually begin to feel a delightful sense of anticipation somewhere in mid-October. But as my time is ruled by the academic term, I also approach it with a certain dread. The beginning of December and the weeks that follow are among the busiest of the year, and I know before I have started that I am likely to miss out on the riches of the readings, antiphons, carols and prayers because I have so little time to stop and relish them. There's always something of a sense of opportunity missed, of time ill spent and of invitation not fully enjoyed and celebrated.

My sense of anticipation before Christmas is also countered by the knowledge that Advent and Christmas are not universally part of everyone's feel-good factor. Many find that Christmas increases any sense of loss or isolation they may already be feeling. Domestic violence always goes up over the Christmas period as families have more time together. Where alcohol, pent-up tensions and simmering anger are in close proximity, this can turn into a powder keg of violence that can explode at any time. Consumer pressure also pushes debt up within families when it's believed that love is proved by spending, so that parents feel obliged to spend money they don't have on presents their children don't need. This consumer pressure fills me with feelings of outrage when I begin to see mince pies, Christmas puddings and Advent calendars on supermarket shelves in September.

For me, at best, times and seasons are welcome opportunities for marking the wonderful variety and rhythms of the year. When they are hijacked, by-passed or ridden roughshod over by the demands of consumer consciousness gone mad, it fills me with disgust. I post enraged photographs of these ill-timed items on WhatsApp and Facebook and make Grumpy Old Woman comments to my patient friends, while ranting about the pointlessness of so-called Advent calendars, which, instead of being a means of increasing anticipation of Christmas through delayed gratification, are simply another excuse to turn the season into a bloated consumer fest.

I have a sense of God rolling divine eyes at me every year. 'Not on about that again, are you? Do you still not understand that I'm willing to take anything I can get on the part of humanity, even if it's the barest remnants of Christian folk memory?' The fourteenth-century English mystic Julian of Norwich claimed remarkably that God is grateful when we remember him. This seems a shocking thing to assert. It sounds as if God is somehow content to take the crumbs off our table. Surely that can't be true?

Yet we have ample evidence from the words and behaviour of Jesus, the Word made flesh, that this is exactly how God is with us. He takes the clumsy faith of a tax collector hidden up a tree, the reticent hope of a Roman centurion unsure of his welcome, the thanks of the one grateful leper and the despairing prayers of a woman outcast and shamed by her defiling illness, and transforms them into life-changing gifts of grace. Prayer and faith are never performance-related activities, nor are they things that we do for God. They are in themselves gifts that God gives and does for us.

We may think that our own or other people's approach to Christmas covers the bare minimum, but the Christmas story, as it unfolds, is all about God's lavish generosity encountering the meagreness of our poverty and transforming it into gift. Most of the characters in official positions are gloriously unaware of their own limitations. Think of Zechariah, Herod, Caesar Augustus and even the Magi. They are all men of power, but they have no idea or fail to recognise what is happening right beneath their noses. Mary and Elizabeth, Joseph and the shepherds manage rather better, but, like the Magi, each of them also has to undertake a journey that consists in relinquishing set notions of who God is and how God acts in human affairs, accepting that, in this case, they are dealing with the God of surprises.

In nativity plays and Christmas liturgies where real sheep and donkeys appear, they are usually clean, well-behaved, soft-pelted and enchanting. My own experience of riding a donkey or a camel for any length of time is an entirely different matter. During a sabbatical visit to the Holy Land in 2019, I had the great privilege of spending a term at the Tantur Ecumenical Institute, which stands above the checkpoint into Bethlehem. We travelled to St Catherine's Monastery in the Sinai desert and were offered the opportunity to trek up the mountain and watch the sunrise. It seemed a wonderful idea at the time, but I knew my physical limits, so I agreed to ride up the mountain on a camel. I don't think I have ever had a more agonisingly uncomfortable journey, well-padded in the rear though I am. I don't know if, like T.S. Eliot's camels in 'The Journey of the Magi', they were galled and sore-footed, but they were certainly refractory. I came to have a healthy respect for the Magi themselves and an equal respect and sympathy for the heavily pregnant Mary journeying from Nazareth to Bethlehem on her donkey.

It all looks so calm and beautiful on the Christmas cards, but the reality is far harder, more uncomfortable, tedious and painful. I suspect that Advent and Christmas themselves are rather like this for many people. We love the idea, but getting down to it can be daunting for all sorts of reasons. Family dynamics can be tense, financial or social challenges can make what we offer seem paltry in light of the yearly expanding Christmas extravaganza pressed on us by the advertising industry. We want to exhibit faith, hope and love, but they can all waver before the bitter realities on the daily news. Yet I remember a moment, halfway up Mount Sinai, when we got off our camels with distinct relief and crowded into a little bivouac where local people plied us with herbal tea and vastly overpriced snacks. It was so cold that we shivered even though we were packed in like sardines, but there was a real sense of communion and of fellowship as we snatched a few minutes of comfort from one another while the camels groaned and snorted on their knees on the edge of the mountain outside.

My hope is that these reflections might be of use not only for individuals once more setting out on the yearly road to Bethlehem, but also for groups journeying together in the global caravan of half-believers, dogged hopers and random fellow travellers. The themes behind the Christmas story have never seemed as relevant as they do at the time of writing. The political regime in the United States triumphed at the polls with an anti-migrant, us-and-them rhetoric which has distinct echoes of the refusal of hospitality at the inn of Bethlehem. Legislation that would make it easier to kill the unborn, the terminally ill, the frail elderly and the disabled sits uncomfortably well within the story of Herod and his massacre of the innocents, as do the disastrous wars currently raging between Israel and Palestine, Russia and Ukraine, and in Sudan, Myanmar, Yemen and beyond. The failure of many religious leaders to listen to critical questions and to the voice of experience among the faithful is akin to the perturbation felt by 'the whole of Jerusalem' as those on the outside arrive with a message from God whose implications overturn all the comfortable assumptions of those on the inside about how God acts within the world and how religious systems should function. Once again, in our own time, it is the poor, the disregarded and the dispossessed who so often see more clearly than those in power, both secular and sacred, whose privilege can blunt their capacity to see things as they are and imagine how they could be.

Here and now, this Advent, we are invited to saddle up our camels or our donkeys and begin the journey anew. Even if we only get to spend a few minutes a day or a few snatched moments during the general Advent mayhem, God is more generous than we could ever ask or imagine. The scriptures, songs and themes of Advent and Christmas are so rich that we cannot escape being reminded that if we give God a millimetre, then a mile will be taken. Jesus, who fed 5,000 with a few loaves and two fish, will take what crumbs of faith, hope and love we can gather and will make a feast of them. That's why it's worth setting out with our companions and becoming Advent pilgrims in whatever way we can.

WEEK 1

FROM
CAPTIVITY
TO
RECON-
CILIATION

Liberated captive

1 December

Isaiah 52:1–2, 7–10

Awake, awake,
*   put on your strength, O Zion;*
put on your beautiful garments,
*   O Jerusalem, the holy city;*
for there shall no more come into you
*   the uncircumcised and the unclean.*
Shake yourself from the dust, arise,
*   O captive Jerusalem;*
loose the bonds from your neck,
*   O captive daughter of Zion…*
How beautiful upon the mountains
*   are the feet of him who brings good tidings,*
who publishes peace, who brings good tidings of good,
*   who publishes salvation,*
*   who says to Zion, 'Your God reigns.'*
Hark, your watchmen lift up their voice,
*   together they sing for joy;*
for eye to eye they see
*   the return of the Lord to Zion.*
Break forth together into singing,
*   you waste places of Jerusalem;*
for the Lord has comforted his people,
*   he has redeemed Jerusalem.*
The Lord has bared his holy arm
*   before the eyes of all the nations;*
and all the ends of the earth shall see
*   the salvation of our God.*

I am an unashamed, absolute lover of Christmas and anything seasonal between Christmas and Candlemas. I remember visiting Oberammergau in Austria some years ago and finding there a shop that sold nothing but Christmas decorations all year round. It was definitely my sort of place.

But much as I love Christmas itself, it's completely overshadowed for me by Advent, even when that season engenders the anxiety that I'm not going to be able to dig out enough time to get the most out of it. Even despite those fears, somehow the anticipation is better than the event itself. This is unusual, as I'm not a particularly patient person, and don't in general take kindly to waiting. But the waiting of Advent is a very special process. The more we inhabit that waiting time and space, the more our capacity grows for receiving what we're waiting for. The wonderful Advent scriptures, hymns and carols speak not only of people but the whole of creation waiting in joyful anticipation for Emmanuel, God with us.

The prophet Isaiah calls on the 'captive daughter of Zion' to wake up as a powerful metaphor for Jerusalem's restoration, redemption and renewal after the disaster of the Babylonian exile. It's a call to spiritual and national renewal, urging Jerusalem to wake up from the despair and inertia caused by suffering and to recognise that God's salvation is coming. Isaiah's encouragement to the daughter of Zion to put on her strength and her beautiful garments is a promise of the renewal of her dignity. Jerusalem will no longer be shamed but, in shaking herself from the dust, will rise from humiliation and reclaim her honour.

Although this prophecy has a particular historical context in the return from long exile, Christians see it as foreshadowing Jesus, the Messiah who would bring spiritual renewal to Israel and the whole world in his gift of ultimate redemption to God's people. When Jesus began his public ministry in his hometown of Nazareth, he read from Isaiah 61 in the synagogue:

'The Spirit of the Lord is upon me,
because he has anointed me to preach good news to the poor.

He has sent me to proclaim release to the captives
and recovering of sight to the blind,
to set at liberty those who are oppressed,
to proclaim the acceptable year of the Lord.'
LUKE 4:18–19

This carries strong echoes of Isaiah 52, with its invitation to loosen the bonds of captivity and embrace a new life and righteousness through faith in God. The prophecy depicts God purifying the holy city, and we remember Jesus driving the money changers out of the temple and promising to raise up the destroyed temple of his body in three days (John 2:13–22). Both the prophecy of Isaiah and the proclamation of the good news by Jesus are also summed up in the book of Revelation:

Then I saw a new heaven and a new earth; for the first heaven and the first earth had passed away, and the sea was no more. And I saw the holy city, new Jerusalem, coming down out of heaven from God, prepared as a bride adorned for her husband; and I heard a loud voice from the throne saying, 'Behold, the dwelling of God is with men. He will dwell with them, and they shall be his people, and God himself will be with them; he will wipe away every tear from their eyes, and death shall be no more, neither shall there be mourning nor crying nor pain any more, for the former things have passed away.'
REVELATION 21:1–4

With the Daughter of Zion, we are invited during Advent to make the journey from captivity to glory, as the coming of Jesus invites us and the whole world to wake up and seize the spiritual freedom and renewal that he promises, of which the New Jerusalem is the final, glorious fulfilment of the whole purpose of creation. Advent seems to reconnect us with the material world, the cosmos itself, in a constant state of hope for a fulfilment that's yet to come. The fact that it hasn't come yet isn't bad news of frustration, or blighted promise, but good news of our capacity for growth. That capacity is what fuels our desire for God, and the waiting can actually increase our capacity.

The French philosopher Emmanuel Levinas denied the role of the divine, but he spoke of this desire for something beyond ourselves as being 'a distance more precious than contact, a non-possession more precious than possession, a hunger that nourishes itself not with bread but with hunger itself'.[1] How can being hungry be better than being satisfied, or distance be better than contact? Perhaps because it's only when we receive the grace truly to know our need of God that a space gets hollowed out in our lives that only God can fill.

Most of us don't see or experience ourselves as captive, but there's a huge industry out there offering to help people overcome bad habits like smoking, overeating, overuse of alcohol and other substances. There are life coaches and therapists by the thousand offering support for those who want to realign their lives, their relationships, their attitude to work, sleep, social media use and other aspects of life that feel out of kilter. Christmas mirrors this for us. It can get full of stuff – presents we don't want or need, rituals that have got tired, family tensions that flare up when we are all corralled together. Advent reminds us of how God can fill the tired and empty spaces within us or help to empty the overfilled ones, if only we are willing to empty them of the junk that often fills them.

Christmas advertisements ask: 'What do you give the person who has everything?' The only answer can be 'Nothing.' It can be a significant liberation to let go of the insecurities that lead us to cling to status, material success and other markers of having made it in life. Christmas is a time of paradoxes and apparent contradictions, the king of kings born in a stable, the greatest news in human history brought to the least important people. In Christmas terms, the best way to become rich lies in learning how to be poor by discovering how to long for what we can never fully grasp. The greatest gift we can ask for is a longing for God and the wisdom to recognise our captivities, great and small, and to learn the courage to let go of our fears and insecurities and embrace the glorious freedom of the followers of the Christ who became poor so that we could be enriched.

-

REFLECTION

- If Isaiah's prophecy were addressed to you personally, what would waking up mean specifically?
- Is there anything in you that feels captive that you long for God to set free?
- Can you name any particular hopes or longings within your heart for yourself or for the world? Take time in whatever way works best for you to share these with God.

-

PRAYER

Loving God, your saving power sets us free from all that holds us captive. Help us this Advent to wake up to the grace you offer and put on the strength that is your gift, so that we can prepare in joy for the coming of your Son. Amen.

Becoming reconciled

2 December

Psalm 46

God is our refuge and strength,
a very present help in trouble.
Therefore we will not fear though the earth should change,
though the mountains shake in the heart of the sea;
though its waters roar and foam,
though the mountains tremble with its tumult.

There is a river whose streams make glad the city of God,
the holy habitation of the Most High.
God is in the midst of her, she shall not be moved;
God will help her right early.
The nations rage, the kingdoms totter;
he utters his voice, the earth melts.
The Lord of hosts is with us;
the God of Jacob is our refuge.

Come, behold the works of the Lord,
how he has wrought desolations in the earth.
He makes wars cease to the end of the earth;
he breaks the bow, and shatters the spear,
he burns the chariots with fire!
'Be still, and know that I am God.
I am exalted among the nations,
I am exalted in the earth!'
The Lord of hosts is with us;
the God of Jacob is our refuge.

The image in the Sistine Chapel of God creating the sun and moon is not for the faint-hearted. God points authoritatively in both directions, patriarchal beard bristling and a look of wrathful determination on his face that could melt the flesh off our bones. Trying to create planets might well give one a rather concentrated cast of countenance, but this portrait looks like the God of judgement that many inwardly believe in while paying lip service to the God of kindness and mercy. This is God the lawmaker who watches and judges our every thought and deed, punishing every infraction, however small. The idea of this God coming close to us is not a happy one, and few people would find the idea of taking refuge here a comforting thought.

After an extended and brutal period of conflict in Gaza and beyond, some may find it uncomfortable to read the psalmist's confident words about God's sovereign power emanating from Zion, the city of God. The Sistine image seems to express this exercise of power to maximum effect, but while Psalm 46 sings of the sovereignty of God over the whole earth, it is not a sovereignty of brutality and force. God is portrayed as ruling with a power which arbitrates definitively between warring nations – the kind of power many of our modern-day populist leaders can only dream of. But God rules according to a criteria of peace rather than aggression, and it is a peace which is not manipulative and based on self-interest, but a transformative power aimed at changing the fundamental dynamics of human relationships. We are invited to be still and know God. It's an invitation to know who it truly is that has creation in hand, an invitation to move from the enthroning of the ego or of one particular nation, culture or ideology to the confident acknowledgment that God is at the heart of everything. This puts into perspective human plans of petty conquest and leads to true freedom.

St Augustine of Hippo, who knew what it was to struggle with his inner demons, writes frequently about true freedom being found in obedience to God's will. He argues that human will is only truly free when it aligns with God's righteousness, because sin corrupts the will and leads to enslavement, whereas serving God in righteousness leads to true freedom: 'A man who is the slave of his passions is not free. But when he begins to serve God, he lays down the yoke of servitude and takes up the yoke of freedom.'[2] This is the inner freedom that gives us confidence whatever is happening in the world or in our own lives. Jesus does not promise that his followers will have an easy life – quite the opposite, in fact. But as he himself faces a cruel death and the apparent failure of his entire ministry, he reassures his disciples, 'I have said this to you, that in me you may have peace. In the world you have tribulation; but be of good cheer, I have overcome the world' (John 16:33).

This confidence in God, despite trial and tribulation, is central to the vision of the Rose Castle Foundation in Cumbria in the north of England. It houses a remarkable community dedicated to interfaith peace-making. Young people from nations and faith communities in conflict from all around the world come to learn the 'twelve habits of a reconciler'. Reconciliation is one of those glib religious terms which rise easily to the lips but often fail to land firmly in our hearts and find expression in our daily interactions. The Rose Castle habits are: hospitality, curiosity, generosity, empathy, vulnerability, humility, forgiveness, lament, gratitude, hope, stewardship and creativity. The idea is that learning to internalise and practise these virtues, or habits, helps us as individuals to bring about reconciliation within society.

The daily practice of any one of these virtues on a personal, let alone an international, basis is a daunting challenge. But the psalmist has no doubt that the bedrock of God's law is the gift of grace given to each one of us to become a practitioner of reconciliation, to learn to be still and to become an instrument of peace. *Hospitality* entails embracing whoever is other with openness and generosity, recognising our shared humanity despite differences. *Curiosity* encourages us to cultivate a deep desire to understand differing perspectives and experiences, so that we can become more open to them. This and all the other habits require the *generosity* on our part to be open-minded and open-hearted without expecting anything in return. We learn *empathy* when we step into another's experience so as genuinely to come to understand their feelings and viewpoints. All of this requires of us a level of *vulnerability*, a willingness to open ourselves emotionally, accepting the possibility of discomfort for the sake of genuine connection with the other. We begin this from a basis of *humility*, maintaining a balanced sense of self while acknowledging our own strengths and limitations.

One of the aims of these habits is to come to a place of understanding and *forgiveness*. Some of those who come to Rose Castle come from places of agonising conflict and have suffered personal loss and trauma. Forgiveness doesn't come easily to any of us. It's a lifelong process, part of which is *lament*, recognising and mourning injustices and suffering, both personally and in the wider world. That truthfulness is a necessary step towards letting go of grudges and resentment and fostering healing and restoration. The fruit of this healing is *gratitude* in which we learn to appreciate the goodness received from others and from God. This experience leads us to learn and nurture within ourselves and our societies the virtue of *hope* as we come to believe in the possibility of positive change and strive towards it.

The final habits of a reconciler are *stewardship* and *creativity*. Creativity enables us to engage in imaginative processes to develop new solutions and expressions that promote reconciliation. We do all this because of our fundamental belief that God has made us partners with all creation, so that we can learn responsibly to manage our gifts, resources and environment for the benefit of all.

The 1972 song 'Peace Will Come', by protest singer Tom Paxton, includes a call for peace to start 'with me'. We tend to prefer thinking that it's others who need to change rather than ourselves, but, like most things, peace is built brick by brick, step by step in the hearts and lives of ordinary people. The psalm makes a direct correlation between our own inner stillness and the breaking of patterns of aggression throughout creation. What happens in the depth of our hearts has resonances beyond our own small sphere. During Advent, God invites us each year to take a few small steps in whatever transformative mind set and practice we are called to at this time. This is how all relationships are built up or destroyed. And as we know from the moon landings, one small step for a human being can become one giant step for humankind.

–

REFLECTION

- Find an image of the painting of God creating the sun and moon from the Sistine Chapel. How does God look there to you? Is this a God that you recognise, either from your own personal image or that of others? What would you like to say to this God? How does this image contrast with the baby in the manger? What feelings and prayers arise in you as you contrast the two?
- Look at the list of the Rose Castle habits of a reconciler (**rosecastlefoundation.org/habits**). Which ones appeal to you most? Which do you find most difficult to practise and why?
- Take time to think about what you most need in light of today's reading and ask God for the grace you most desire.

–

PRAYER

Loving God, as we set out on our Advent journey, fill our hearts with the desire to walk in your paths and learn your ways. Give us the grace we need to build relationships of peace and reconciliation, one step at a time. Amen.

Making the journey

3 December

Luke 5:17–26 (NRSV)

One day while he was teaching, Pharisees and teachers of the law who had come from every village of Galilee and Judea and from Jerusalem were sitting nearby, and the power of the Lord was with him to heal. Just then some men came carrying a paralysed man on a stretcher. They were trying to bring him in and lay him before Jesus, but, finding no way to bring him in because of the crowd, they went up on the roof and let him down on the stretcher through the tiles into the middle of the crowd in front of Jesus. When he saw their faith, he said, 'Friend, your sins are forgiven you.' Then the scribes and the Pharisees began to question, 'Who is this who is speaking blasphemies? Who can forgive sins but God alone?' When Jesus perceived their questionings, he answered them, 'Why do you raise such questions in your hearts? Which is easier: to say, "Your sins are forgiven you," or to say, "Stand up and walk"? But so that you may know that the Son of Man has authority on earth to forgive sins' – he said to the one who was paralysed – 'I say to you, stand up and take your stretcher and go to your home.' Immediately he stood up before them, took what he had been lying on, and went to his home, glorifying God. Amazement seized all of them, and they glorified God and were filled with fear, saying, 'We have seen incredible things today.'

This is a wonderful, if quirky, scene to imagine: the awkwardness of the climb with the stretcher and its human burden in tow, the taking apart of the roof, the wrath of the householder, the precarious swinging of the stretcher on its ropes as it is lowered by the man's friends, staring down through the hole they have made, the Pharisees in their self-righteous anger, the people in their amazement. And what of Jesus and the paralysed man himself? It's a story of relationships and encounters, as are most of the stories from the gospels.

Above all, it's a story of faith, hope and love being a joint enterprise. The man's faith and hope are part of the faith and hope of his friends – they cannot exist separately from one another and are proof of their love and the power of friendship. Faith is simultaneously deeply private but essentially communal. We worship in our hearts but also within the faith community, where our faith and also our doubts and hesitations, pooled together, can become something life-giving. Above all, community can be the nursery in which the seeds of friendship take root and bear fruit in love.

When we are baptised, we are baptised into a new mode of being human, becoming a new person in Christ for whom the usual social categories of human hierarchy no longer exist. Paul tells us that when we are in Christ, we can no longer identify ourselves in the first instance as Jew or Gentile, slave or free, male or female (Galatians 3:28). These were the primary categories of social differentiation in his time, which pointed to an automatic sense of ascending or descending value in the human person. But the liberating message brought to us by a baby born so poor that he was a homeless refugee, lying in a cattle trough after his birth amid the messy chaos, smell and dirt of a stable, is that each of us has the supreme value of being made in God's own image, irrespective of any identifying categories or the circumstances of our birth. As Herod found out to his cost, God is no respecter of persons and is not impressed by titles and what passes among us for prestige or privilege.

Whenever Jesus meets someone who has truly taken in that they are a child of God, seeking and doing the Father's will, whatever their origin, he recognises them as a sister or brother. Most crucially for Christian witness, he invites us to do the same. Great Christian saints have always done this: while accounts that St Vincent de Paul personally took up the oars among the galley slaves to whom he was appointed chaplain by Louis XIII of France are probably legend, he advocated passionately for their better treatment and worked, despite opposition, to secure their release.

Elizabeth Fry was shocked by the terrible conditions of women and children crammed together without proper food or clothing in Newgate Prison in London and helped create the Association for the Reformation of the Female Prisoners in Newgate in 1817. It became a model for prison reform worldwide and inspired future penal reformers. Her Quaker faith also inspired her to establish night shelters for London's homeless and to work for the improvement of conditions in workhouses and provide schooling for poor children.

Gladys Aylward was a domestic servant who felt called to be a missionary in China but was rejected by the China Inland Mission due to her lack of formal education. In 1930, she made a dangerous journey on her own to China via Siberia and, once there, worked with an elderly missionary running an inn for mule drivers and sharing the gospel with travellers. She adopted Chinese customs, learned the language, and was eventually accepted by the local people and appointed by the Chinese government as a foot-binding inspector, helping to end the practice of binding women's feet which made them so small that they could not walk properly. She also spread Christian teachings and became a trusted mediator in local disputes, following the model of biblical justice. When Japan invaded China in 1938, Aylward took responsibility for over 100 orphaned children, leading them on a dangerous 300-mile journey over the mountains to safety, relying on her faith and praying constantly for guidance and protection despite exhaustion and injury. She is remembered for her unwavering faith, courage and devotion to the people of China despite facing immense hardships. They found in this overlooked and underestimated English woman an unexpected friend.

Nearer our own time, we see countless people all over the world offering their time and service in response to their faith, volunteering in situations of terrible deprivation and working alongside local people to help them achieve a life of dignity and a future full of hope, while also learning from them the ways of true human solidarity.

The Christmas story is also about finding friends in unexpected places: men of wisdom and power worshipping as equals alongside peasants; those at the inn who took pity on a desperate young couple from out of town; shepherds, outcast from synagogue worship by virtue of their profession, being brought into the very presence of God-with-us to worship directly, in spirit and in truth. Our Advent reflection finds us in a gospel story about a journey of faith, hope and love, even if this particular camel trek only takes us as far as the roof of a house. From the glimmerings of faith in some hopeful, house-breaking friends to its confirmation in forgiveness and healing is an epic journey which is made one step at a time, impelled by a passion for the common good. It's a journey that we make best in a community of friends.

–

REFLECTION

- Take time to imagine this gospel scene in all its practical details, experiencing the feelings and reactions of any or all of the actors within the scene. What do you most notice? What feelings do you experience as you contemplate the scene?
- Are there any particular heroes of faith, hope and love who have inspired you? What is it in these people that you most admire?
- Many of us have prayed for the healing of those we love, only for our prayer apparently not to be granted. Is there anything you want to say to Jesus about this? What do you imagine that he wants to say back? Take time for a conversation or just to hold out your deep needs and desires before him.

–

PRAYER

Lord Jesus, you came into our world to heal our wounds and to take away the sin of the world, which can hurt and trouble us so deeply. Help us today to experience your healing love and to have confidence that you will make our lives fruitful, whatever our circumstances. Amen.

Forgiveness   4 December

Matthew 18:12–14

'What do you think? If a man has a hundred sheep, and one of them has gone astray, does he not leave the ninety-nine on the mountains and go in search of the one that went astray? And if he finds it, truly, I say to you, he rejoices over it more than over the ninety-nine that never went astray. So it is not the will of my Father who is in heaven that one of these little ones should perish.'

Is your general life experience that of being one of the ninety-nine sheep or the one who went astray? Both roles have their advantages and their challenges. If you were a 'good' girl or boy, you will have avoided the painful scenes, conversations and recriminations that accompany the bad boy or girl role. No being put in the corner or on the naughty step for you. No being sent to bed with no supper or put into detention. No feeling that you can never get it right, even when you do actually try. Parents, teachers and other adults in roles of authority will have looked on you with approval, siblings will have been encouraged to look to you as a good example and the parents of schoolmates will have been happy to have you round to their house as a Suitable Friend.

So much for the advantages. The disadvantage is that when things do go wrong in later life, even – and perhaps especially – when it's trouble not of your own making, it can come as a tremendous shock. This is Not How Things Should Be. Experience has taught you that good behaviour, or at least good intentions, bring their own reward, but suddenly the cause and effect of good behaviour and reward doesn't work anymore – the rules of the game seem to have shifted, and life no longer works out the way that you expect. History is full of examples of virtuous and well-meaning people getting caught up in trouble despite their best efforts. This can feel terribly unfair. It can also prove bitterly hard when people who are used to being on the right side of things do make mistakes and suffer or cause others to suffer as a consequence. They never meant things to turn out like this, and they can find it devastating to face and deal with and impossible to believe that they can truly be forgiven.

Whether we carry the good or bad child image within us, many of us carry negative tapes in our heads: if only I had or hadn't; I should; I shouldn't; I ought; I must… It's what has been called 'hardening of the oughteries'. In these scenarios, approval or reward are always dependent on our efforts and are only given if we conform to someone else's rules, whereas punishment is always lurking to pounce on us for misdemeanours that are always entirely our own fault. There is a terrible sense of let down or betrayal if the rule of virtue bringing reward doesn't work or if the rules appear to change.

'Bad' girls or boys sense that such rules are unreliable and have rebelled against them from an early age. The apparent advantages of being free from adult restraint and an externally imposed framework of behaviour can seem like a benefit, but they also carry their own negative connotations. They can lead to a cynicism that is corrosive of a healthy self-belief: what's the point of trying; no one will ever give me credit anyway; I'll never match up to whoever the paragon of good behaviour is; I'll always be identified by my worst deeds or habits; I always; I never…

In all the encounters we read of in the gospels, Jesus seems to have had an instinctive knowledge of the type of person he was dealing with. We don't know if Mary of Bethany was a 'bad girl', but we know that her sister Martha suffered from all the anxieties and inner constraints of the 'good girl' trying desperately to get everything right (Luke 10:38–42). He understands and makes space for the needs of both, as well as offering them opportunities for growth. He equally understands the need of Matthew and Zacchaeus to have their capacity for humility, generosity and hospitality recognised, while also not avoiding or allowing them to avoid acknowledging the shadier side of their lives.

Many commentators have interpreted Jesus' encounter with the woman of Samaria in John's gospel (John 4:1–42) as a conversation with a fallen woman, just as Mary Magdalene has been cast in art and in much spiritual literature as a former prostitute. There is no biblical evidence for this. We are told that Mary Magdalene had seven demons cast out of her, but that was a way that people in biblical times described a whole variety of ills, not necessarily involving sexual sin. Jesus tells the Samaritan woman that she has had five husbands and that her current partner is not married to her. But we know that it was extremely difficult for Samaritan or Jewish women of that era to instigate divorce proceedings, whereas a man could divorce his wife because she had grown unattractive or was unable to produce children (it was always assumed to be the woman's fault) or because he didn't like her cooking. If the woman was on her sixth partner, it may have been because the previous ones had died or repudiated her. Hers is more likely to be a story of repeated tragedy, rather than of repeated guilt. Jesus defies all social and cultural norms to meet her questions and her search for an understanding of God beyond the limits of what life and her own culture have taught her. He is the living embodiment of God with us not as a restrictive imposer of rules but as life-giver, meeting us in spirit and truth.

The story of the shepherd and the ninety-nine sheep doesn't say that God is not interested in those who manage easily to be good, but it does offer reassurance that whenever we fail, or life fails us, he will always be at our side as God-with-us. Nothing we could ever do, think or say and nothing that befalls us can come between us and the love of God in Christ Jesus. The prophecies foretelling Christ's coming reassure us of this, as do the details of the story of his birth. This is what we are invited to remember and take to heart during Advent.

–

REFLECTION

- Do you generally see yourself as well or badly behaved, a saint or a sinner? What image of yourself does that leave you with, as a rule?
- How do you think God looks on you? Is God's love for you dependent on your good behaviour?
- If you have any memories of repenting or of God seeking and finding you when lost, what was that like? If not, can you imagine such a situation?
- How does it feel to have God rejoice in finding you and bringing you home?

–

PRAYER

Jesus, our loving shepherd, you were welcomed into this world by shepherds, who knew what it was to lose, seek and find lost sheep. Help us to trust that you will always come in search of us if we get lost or lose sight of you through the circumstances of our life. Help us to remember that there will always be a welcome home for us. Amen.

Hungry for God

5 December

Now when Jesus heard this, he withdrew from there in a boat to a lonely place apart. But when the crowds heard it, they followed him on foot from the towns. As he went ashore he saw a great throng; and he had compassion on them, and healed their sick. When it was evening, the disciples came to him and said, 'This is a lonely place, and the day is now over; send the crowds away to go into the villages and buy food for themselves.' Jesus said, 'They need not go away; you give them something to eat.' They said to him, 'We have only five loaves here and two fish.' And he said, 'Bring them here to me.' Then he ordered the crowds to sit down on the grass; and taking the five loaves and the two fish he looked up to heaven, and blessed, and broke and gave the loaves to the disciples, and the disciples gave them to the crowds. And they all ate and were satisfied. And they took up twelve baskets full of the broken pieces left over. And those who ate were about five thousand men, besides women and children.

Recently the Vatican revised its directives to bishops on what to do if someone claimed to be receiving revelations or visions from God. Couched in the Latin of canon law, the responses are cautious and range, in so many words, from 'so far so reasonably credible' to 'not a hope of being considered true'. The internet is full of claims of divine revelation, like the assertion of Florida resident Diana Duyser in 1994 that the Virgin Mary had appeared in silhouette in her grilled cheese sandwich. The sandwich remained uncorrupted for ten years, and Duyser finally sold it on eBay for $28,000. When the new Vatican directives were published a spokeswoman was interviewed about them and asked what kinds of claims the Vatican was currently processing. She cited the case of a woman who insisted that Jesus was appearing in her kitchen and multiplying pizzas.

The gospels tell a story which, in the first instance, sounds barely more credible. All four gospel writers describe the feeding of the multitude with a few loaves and fish. We have various choices as to how we receive and interpret this story. Some have offered pragmatic interpretations which have Jesus calling on the crowds to share what they have brought with friend or stranger. This inspires his listeners to a generosity they would not otherwise have felt, and from the plenty of the few, everyone is eventually fed. This has resonances for us today. Most of the supermarkets in the UK now carry special bins and posters advertising the local food bank for which shoppers can donate a little extra for those who are unable to feed themselves and their families on a reliable basis. Food banks, baby banks for clothes, nappies and baby food, and other charitable schemes of sharing and exchange sadly have become a necessary feature of modern life, but they flourish through people's sense of solidarity. Even if we are not people with lots to spare, a modest gift, when given by many, can result in enough to feed a city.

Many families now operate a reverse Advent calendar. Instead of the ones which simply extend the Christmas consumer indulgence over an extra month by offering 24 days' worth of luxury goodies, each day has an item for buying and donating to the local food bank or charity centre. This is a lovely reminder of the God who wanted to enter every aspect of our human lives, sharing our poverty and our need and offering us a pattern of self-gift and imaginative generosity. The 'Secret Santa' and other anonymous gifting traditions operate in workplaces all over the world. The anonymity carries resonances of Jesus' words in Luke 6, where he speaks of giving or lending without hope of return. If we are only good to those who are good to us, where is the virtue in that? Being good to someone anonymously is another way of sharing the generosity of God, who gave the greatest treasure the world has ever known to people who might never recognise it for what it was.

Other biblical interpreters don't hesitate to accept a miraculous interpretation of the multiplication of the loaves. If Jesus can heal the blind, the lame and the dying, he can surely provide food for the hungry. But there is more to this story than a miraculous answer to a pressing practical problem. The story urges us to look at what we hunger and thirst for. In the beatitudes Jesus blesses those who hunger and thirst for justice or righteousness (Matthew 5:6). When he himself is hungry and is tempted by Satan to turn stones into bread, he reminds the tempter that human beings do not live on bread alone but on every word that comes from God (Matthew 4:4). How many of us actually hunger or thirst, or have a similar sense of longing and need, for God's word, and what does it mean to nourish ourselves on it?

There are many methods of meditating on the scriptures. One of the oldest is *lectio divina*. Latin for 'divine reading', it is a traditional Christian practice of prayerfully reading and meditating on scripture, not simply studying the text but encountering God through his word. This method has been practised since the early church and was formally developed by St Benedict in the sixth century. Later it was promoted by Guigo II, a Carthusian monk of the twelfth century, who outlined the four key steps of *lectio divina*:

1 *Lectio* (Reading) – What does the text say? We choose a short passage from scripture and read it slowly, attentively and repeatedly, noticing words or phrases that stand out. These may be what God is bringing to our attention.

2 *Meditatio* (Meditation) – What does this text say to me? We reflect on the passage and how it applies to our life, asking: what is God saying to me personally here? We can use our imagination, placing ourselves in the scene if it's a gospel or other story.

3 *Oratio* (Prayer) – What do I want to say to God? We respond to God by praying from the heart, sharing our thoughts, struggles, desires or gratitude, asking God to deepen our understanding and transform us.

4   *Contemplatio* (Contemplation) – How is God drawing me closer?
    We rest in God's presence, allowing the words to sink into our soul
    beyond thoughts and words, simply being with God, embracing
    his love and guidance.

Some traditions add a fifth step, *Actio* (Action), which focuses on how
I live this out and how the passage inspires a change in my daily life.

Commentators on *lectio* have said that it's 'ruminating' on the word of
God, like a cow chewing the cud to get every last bit of nourishment
from it! It was put simply but succinctly by an old Revivalist preacher
who, when asked how he prepared his sermons, said, 'I reads myself
full, I thinks myself clear, I prays myself hot, and I lets myself go.'

I meet too many people who tell me that they don't know how to pray
and feel depressed by spiritual books which seem to be aimed at people
they could never hope to be. But when they start to talk about what
does go on when they try to pray, I know that I am listening to people
who know quite well how to communicate with God, but don't recognise that this is what they are doing. They are convinced that prayer is
some mystical and spooky specialist skill, reserved to professionally
'holy' people or to God's chosen few.

We are always going to be reduced to nothing when trying to enter the
presence of the living God. God is entirely other, and we are limited
human beings. But we are wired for God; it's in our DNA to long to reach
out or deep within and find the God who, in Meister Eckhart's delightful
description, is like someone behind us who calls to our attention by
clearing their throat. One of the twentieth century's great contempla-
tives, the Trappist monk Thomas Merton, wrote:

> In prayer we discover what we already have. You start from where
> you are and you deepen what you already have, and you realize
> you are already there. We already have everything, but we don't
> know it and don't experience it. Everything has been given to us
> in Christ. All we need is to experience what we already possess.[3]

If we take our hunger seriously, God is only too ready to feed our longing and does it quite simply with the word who came to dwell among us.

–

REFLECTION

- In the beatitudes Jesus calls blessed those who hunger and thirst for justice, and he tells Satan that we don't live on bread alone but on every word that comes from God. If you were to choose some Bible verses to help this message to become more real in your life, what verses would you choose?
- What is it, in spiritual terms, that you hunger and thirst for? Take time to express this to God.

–

PRAYER

Jesus, bread of life, you encourage us to nourish ourselves with your living word. You are the Word made flesh, who came to live among us. We ask for the grace for your word to become alive in us, so that those who encounter us, encounter your word brought to life in us. Amen.

Finding the way

6 December

Matthew 7:21, 24–27

'Not every one who says to me, "Lord, Lord," shall enter the kingdom of heaven, but he who does the will of my Father who is in heaven… Every one then who hears these words of mine and does them will be like a wise man who built his house upon the rock; and the rain fell, and the floods came, and the winds blew and beat upon that house, but it did not fall, because it had been founded on the rock. And every one who hears these words of mine and does not do them will be like a foolish man who built his house upon the sand; and the rain fell, and the floods came, and the winds blew and beat against that house, and it fell; and great was the fall of it.'

In 2021 four huge concrete cooling towers standing 117 metres tall were demolished near Rugely in Staffordshire to make way for over 2,000 homes, a school, park land and employment spaces. The crowd of spectators was so big that it became a public danger, and police had to warn them to stay away and watch the demolition online from home. There is something mesmerising about great structures falling. We can barely believe that something that seemed so solid and permanent can come crashing down and crumble into nothing but rubble and dust.

Jesus uses a similarly dramatic image to describe the flimsiness of faith which consists more in lip service than in living and acting according to God's will. It's a stern warning which leaves us with something of a dilemma. How exactly do we know what God's will is, and how can we be sure that we are doing it?

Many people believe that God has a divine blueprint for each of us, in which every detail of our life has been mapped out beforehand. This God says to us: 'I've got a plan for the whole of your life, all worked out for you, but I'm keeping it a secret. You have to spend your life trying to discover what it is. I won't give you any helpful clues, but I'll punish you forever if you don't figure it out correctly.' This is emphatically not the God revealed to us by Jesus. It's a monster who delights in tormenting us with anxiety and guilt, while making it impossible for us to work out who and how we should be in this world.

Throughout history, Christians have sought ways to understand and follow God's will for their lives in methods ranging from prayer, scripture study, reasoned decision-making in the more formal and theological context, to some quite astonishing folk methods at the more superstitious end of the market. Believers prayerfully reflect on Bible passages and apply them to their lives or pray directly to discern God's will. We see Jesus himself, in Luke 6:12–13, praying all night before choosing his disciples. Proverbs 11:14 says, 'Where there is no guidance, a people falls, but in an abundance of counsellors there is safety.' Many people consult pastors, spiritual directors, or other mature and trusted believers to gain wisdom. In Acts 15 we see the early church making decisions through group discernment and counsel so that, in answer to a question vexing the wider community, the leaders can write confidently: 'For it has seemed good to the Holy Spirit and to us...' (v. 28).

St Thomas Aquinas emphasises using reason alongside faith, teaching that God has given us minds to think and choose wisely, so we should use our reason and common sense. Our decisions should align with scriptural principles, wisdom and moral truth and if a choice clearly contradicts God's commands, it is unlikely to be his will. If a decision leads to deep peace and joy, it is more likely to come from God than if it brings persistent anxiety, turmoil or doubt. Even the subconscious can be a helpful guide when it tries to surface, and throughout scripture we see God guiding people through dreams (Joseph deciding to take Mary as his wife; the Magi being told to avoid returning to Herod), visions (Peter in Acts 10) and signs (Gideon's fleece in Judges 6:36–40).

The *Spiritual Exercises* of St Ignatius of Loyola aim to help people rid themselves of what he calls 'disordered attachments' that can bind us in patterns that are destructive and compulsive. We can be attached to images of God and of ourselves or to relationships or behaviours that are warped and destructive, destroying our sense of our own or another's worth. Ignatius encourages us to counter this by discovering our deepest desires, because this is where God's will also resides.

In this he echoes St Augustine of Hippo, who lived a wild life as a young man. After his conversion he wrote: 'The whole life of a good Christian is holy desire. What you desire you cannot see yet. But the desire gives you the capacity, so that when it does happen that you see, you may be fulfilled... this is our life, to be exercised by desire.'[4] Those words, 'the desire gives you the capacity', point to a direct relationship between our deepest longings and our capacity to have them fulfilled.

Throughout history, people have also sought signs and divine guidance using folk traditions, superstitions and personal rituals. In the Old Testament, people used the Urim and Thummim, sacred stones to cast lots to determine God's will. We see this in Joshua 18:6 and Acts 1:26. Less biblically, people have flipped coins, drawn slips of paper or thrown dice, trusting that God controls the outcome. The Bible flip-and-point method sees people randomly opening the Bible and pointing to a verse, believing it will reveal God's will. There's a joke about a nun who did this and landed on Matthew 27:5: '[Judas] went and hanged himself.' Horrified, she tried again and got Luke 10:37: 'Go and do likewise'!

Some people seek signs, like the man in the story who is trying to decide whether to marry Susie or Maria. He goes into a Catholic church to pray and sees an inscription by a statue of the Virgin Mary that reads 'Ave Maria'. In ancient and medieval times, people observed the movement of stars, the flight patterns of birds, sudden weather changes or seeing a certain animal at the right moment, believing them to be divine messages. Folk methods show how deeply people desire divine guidance, even in creative or unconventional ways. The difficulty with these sorts of method is that they can become a way of manipulating outcomes rather than trusting God's wisdom.

In the book of Revelation Jesus says: 'Listen! I am standing at the door, knocking; if you hear my voice and open the door, I will come in to you and eat with you, and you with me' (Revelation 3:20, NRSV). Many carols feature Mary and Joseph knocking at doors in Bethlehem with no one willing to open the door to them. The famous painting of *The Light of the World* by William Holman Hunt shows Jesus knocking at a door that has been closed for so long that ivy has grown over and all around it. The door has no handle from the outside, it can only be opened from within. We open our hearts to God's will and God's grace in our lives not by making the right holy noises or finding the right method, but by having open hearts, eyes and ears to detect God's presence all around us, and when we act on God's invitation to become words made flesh in our turn. A balanced approach often involves prayer, scripture, wise counsel and careful thought.

God's will is not just about decisions, but about growing in relationship with him. No single method is foolproof, but when spiritual and practical approaches are combined, they can help believers make wise and faithful choices.

–

REFLECTION

- If you can, find a photo of Holman Hunt's *The Light of the World* painting. How does it speak to you? Is there anything you want to say to Jesus as he knocks at your door?
- Find an Advent hymn or Christmas carol that mentions God's longing to be with us and God teaching us how to live and choose well. How does it make you think about finding God's will in your life?

–

PRAYER

Lord Jesus, you called blessed all who do your Father's will and you yourself prayed to do his will and not your own. Help us to seek and find God's will for ourselves, through recognising our deepest desires and offering them to you, our heart's desire. Amen.

Lighten our darkness

7 December

Psalm 27:1, 4, 13–14

The Lord is my light and my salvation;
  whom shall I fear?
The Lord is the stronghold of my life;
  of whom shall I be afraid?…

One thing I have asked of the Lord,
  that I will seek after;
that I may dwell in the house of the Lord
  all the days of my life,
to behold the beauty of the Lord,
  and to inquire in his temple…

I believe that I shall see the goodness of the Lord
  in the land of the living!
Wait for the Lord;
  be strong, and let your heart take courage;
  yea, wait for the Lord!

The difference between light and darkness can be enormous. Children and even adults can be terrified at the thought of 'things that go bump in the night', dangerous or threatening creatures lurking in the dark corners of a room which feels safe and peacefully familiar in the light of day. A harmless pair of slippers under the bed or a slight bulge in the curtains created by a draught can suddenly become a monster or a dangerous intruder waiting to pounce.

There's a much-repeated story about a little boy who was terrified of going to sleep in the dark. His parents had tried everything to comfort and reassure him, but nothing worked. In desperation his father said, 'Don't worry, you won't be alone in the dark, because God will be here looking after you.' He thought he'd made a good point until a little voice wailed back from the bed, 'But I don't want God; I want someone with skin on!'

Jesus came into the world precisely to be God with skin on, taking a body like ours, living a life like ours and dying a death like ours. The dark we fear as adults may not be the physical dark, but what we carry within us. People often talk of doubt as darkness or of the experience of bereavement, breakdown of relationships or unhealed hurts as 'being in a dark place'. Winston Churchill famously described the depression from which he suffered as 'the black dog'. Suffering mental or physical illness can feel like falling down a dark hole into which no light shines.

One of my favourite Advent customs is the one of lighting one more candle each week on the Advent wreath to signify the light of Christ that's coming into the world. An old proverb says, 'It's better to light a candle than curse the darkness.' Each time we reject despair and cynicism in favour of hope, we make the world a brighter and more faith-filled place. Jesus' disciples were happy to follow him in the light, while he was preaching and teaching and working miracles. When he warned them that he would suffer and die, they protested. But the dark times of our lives are precisely when we need a God with skin on.

God doesn't promise us that we will escape the darkness and have a life free of pain, suffering and death. But in Jesus God enters into the darkness with us and promises us that we are never alone. Peter, James and John saw Jesus transfigured in glory on the mountain (Matthew 17:1–6). The night before he died, Jesus led them up the Mount of Olives, where they saw him in his agony (Matthew 26:36–46). The cross and the resurrection, the light and the dark, are two sides of the same coin. Jesus walks beside us in the valley of shadow, and the darkness can never overpower him.

As Advent progresses, the northern hemisphere moves inexorably towards the darkest time of the year, with Christmas itself coming only a few days after the winter solstice, which has the longest night and the shortest amount of daylight. It's not surprising, then, that many of the scriptures connected with the birth of Christ speak of darkness and light. The prophet Isaiah speaks of the people who walked in darkness seeing a great light and of light shining on those who walked in the shadow of death (Isaiah 9:2). John's prologue assures us that the light shines in the darkness, which has not overcome it (John 1:5). When we are indoors, warm, safe and comfortable, it's easy to believe this and even to take it for granted. When we are alone in the dark, whether that darkness is inside or outside us, it is harder to believe in that light which cannot be overcome.

The decision to celebrate Christmas near the winter solstice on 25 December was made for both theological and practical reasons, rather than because someone stood in the stable at Bethlehem with a calendar. The reasons include the date's alignment with pre-Christian solstice festivals, such as Roman Saturnalia (17–23 December), which featured feasting, gift-giving and social role reversals, where slaves could act as masters for a day. This was taken up in later centuries in cathedrals and monasteries, with a choirboy or novice chosen to act temporarily as the bishop or abbot during the Feast of St Nicholas (6 December) or the Feast of the Holy Innocents (28 December). While mainly expressing a social need for relaxation of otherwise rigid hierarchies, this role reversal also reminds us of the humility of the 'God with skin on', who, as Paul reminds us:

> Though he was in the form of God, did not count equality with God a thing to be grasped, but emptied himself, taking the form of a servant, being born in the likeness of men. And being found in human form he humbled himself and became obedient unto death, even death on a cross.
>
> PHILIPPIANS 2:6–8

The theme of God as our light and help also echoes the Roman 'Birthday of the Unconquered Sun', the sun god *Sol Invictus*. Early Christians did not initially celebrate Christmas, but by the fourth century, 25 December had been established as the feast of Christ's birth. Some scholars suggest that the church chose this date to emphasise Jesus as the true 'light of the world' (John 1:5; 8:12) and the light that overcomes darkness (Isaiah 9:2). The *Sol Invictus* festival absorbed older traditions, including the Mithraic cult, popular among Roman soldiers, in which the sun-related deity Mithras was often depicted slaying a bull with the sun shining above him. Church leaders like Pope Leo I (440–461) warned Christians against honouring the sun instead of Christ, even though the theme of Jesus as the 'sun of righteousness' (Malachi 4:2) matched the solstice symbolism.

Other Christian sources suggest that Jesus' birth was calculated independently, based on the idea that he was conceived on 25 March, the Feast of the Annunciation, making 25 December his birth date. This derived from a Jewish belief based on the idea that great figures lived a 'perfect' lifespan and died on the same date as the one on which they were conceived, in different years. Based on the belief that prophets died on the anniversary of their conception, they reasoned that Jesus must have been conceived on the same day he died. The Western Church calculated that date as 25 March, which connected his death to Passover, with his birth exactly nine months later in December. The Eastern Church calculated the crucifixion as 6 April, so this led to a different date for Jesus' birth, 6 January, which became the feast of Epiphany.

All this is interesting background to some of the key Christian dates, but where do such ideas lead us? Psalm 27 opens with fighting words: 'The Lord is my light and my salvation; whom shall I fear? The Lord is the stronghold of my life; of whom shall I be afraid?' These words are easily said, but not always easily acted on or felt. We can be like children playing at going on a bear hunt and chanting proudly, 'I'm not scared', only to think that we see eyes and snout and claws at the back of the cave and run all the way home. Yet the Psalms were written at a time when life was precarious for most people, when straying outside safe boundaries and even sometimes staying within them was a risky business. Wild animals lurked, enemies advanced, natural disasters could not be avoided and, as another psalm notes, plagues could lay waste at noon.

But Psalm 27 roots its confidence in two things: living in the house of the Lord and hope. Most of us can't and wouldn't even wish to live in a temple or church, but we can find the temple within. Our homes can become holy places if we develop and nurture a sense of God with us in our everyday lives. Learning to savour and appreciate the little things of life as God's gifts to us can help us to 'behold the beauty of the Lord'. Hope is not the same as optimism. It faces reality but insists that change is possible. It believes that Christ has already overcome sin and death, therefore we can have confidence that suffering and evil never have the final say. Even in the dead of winter darkness, that is what will help us to hold firm and take heart.

-

REFLECTION

- Is there anything in your life at present that causes you to fear or lose heart? How might you speak to God about this?
- Advent is a special time to make decorations and crafts that play with light. If you don't have time to do this, you could simply light an Advent candle in the darkness. What thoughts and prayers come to you as you see light shining in the dark?

-

PRAYER

Jesus, you are the light that no darkness can ever overcome. Shine your light in the dark places of our minds and hearts, in the darkness of our world, and help us to hold firm and take heart. Amen.

WEEK 2

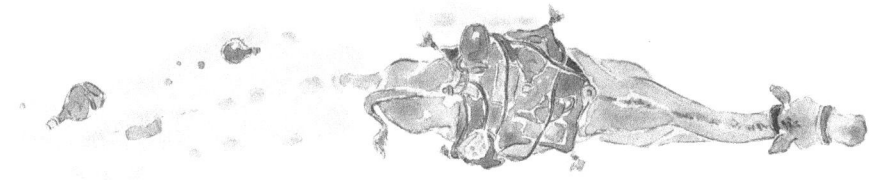

THE
TRANS-
FORMING
POWER
OF GOD'S
PRESENCE

'Who is my mother?'

8 December

Matthew 12:46–49

While he was still speaking to the people, behold, his mother and his brothers stood outside, asking to speak to him. But he replied to the man who told him, 'Who is my mother, and who are my brothers?' And stretching out his hand towards his disciples, he said, 'Here are my mother and my brothers!'

For Roman Catholics, 8 December is a special date, celebrated as the Feast of the Immaculate Conception of the Virgin Mary. This is an old doctrine, dating back to the very early church, which struggled to accept that Jesus was both truly God and truly human. There was a prevailing belief that all human beings inherited the sin of Adam and Eve, so how could God be born of sin? The theological answer to this conundrum was the belief that, through the saving merits of Jesus, Mary, the human mother of whom he was born, was herself conceived without sin. Different theologians disagreed about this down the centuries, but the doctrine finally became official teaching.

Mary remains a controversial figure in the sometimes-strained relations between Christians of different traditions. Catholic and Orthodox Christians address prayers and hymns to her that call her Mother of God, Queen of Apostles and Gate of Heaven, while for many Protestant Christians, these titles sound not only excessive but theologically wrong – Jesus Christ alone is the way, the truth and the life. They point to what they see as the lack of scriptural basis for the dogmas and devotions that have arisen around Mary during two millennia of Christian history. While she is significantly present at the beginning and the end of Jesus' public ministry in John's gospel, Jesus made no great claims on behalf of his mother, and indeed taught that he himself was the only mediator between humankind and his heavenly Father.

Within her own family, Mary proved a disputed figure – the gospels tell of how Joseph struggled to believe that her child was not born of sin (Matthew 1:19). Opinion is divided even within the Catholic Church, where there is a long tradition of contrasting Eve, the sinner and temptress, with Mary, the perfectly pure and submissive virgin and mother. Feminists argue that this is an unhelpful role model, the source of an idealisation of female modesty that leaves no room for autonomy, self-fulfilment and healthy sexuality. The Latin tradition of the sorrowful mother has been accused by political radicals of engendering a religious fatalism aimed at keeping the poor in their place.

But a closer look at the scriptures and at the Marian tradition leads us to an understanding of Christian discipleship for women and men that can fully engage all our human responses with God's grace. Seen in this way, Mary is not a source of division but one in whom we can all find inspiration for faithful discipleship and a total response to God's gracious call.

The Bible presents Mary as the archetypal disciple, the human being in whom we see, as in a mirror, all that we can be and become through the power of God, despite our human doubts and weakness. At the annunciation Mary questions the angel Gabriel, and she continues to ask awkward questions of God, as many of us do in our struggle to understand God's ways: 'How can this be?'; 'Why have you done this?' At Cana and during his public ministry, Jesus does not single his mother out for honour because of her biological role but responds to her as someone who hears God's word and gives it flesh and bones. Like all the disciples of Jesus, Mary in the gospels walks by faith and not by sight. She treasures what words she has received of Jesus, 'pondering them in her heart' (Luke 2:19).

Orthodox icons of the dormition or assumption of Mary tell of the belief that at her death Mary was taken up body and soul into heaven, a foretaste of the resurrection of the body that all Christians look towards in the Apostles' Creed. Where pictures of the nativity typically show Mary cradling the body of her baby Son, wrapped in swaddling clothes, pictures of the dormition show Jesus cradling in his arms the body and soul of his mother, wrapped in a shroud as she is born into everlasting life. Her body also appears like that of a baby, but such pictures express the belief that all human experience, body and soul, is destined for glory through the saving power of Jesus. Prayers from the Orthodox and Catholic traditions call Mary the God-bearer, whose child is the Saviour, but as we read in Luke's gospel, she had to learn the meaning of this for herself.

Mary stands for a fundamental Protestant understanding of a human in relationship with their creator, encountering God in unmediated fashion. She stands for all of us, not because she is an extraordinary human being, but because human beings are extraordinary. God loves, trusts and cooperates with us. This is expressed in dramatic fashion by Bernard of Clairvaux (1090–1153) in one of his most famous Advent homilies. He depicts the whole of creation holding its breath and waiting for Mary's answer to the angel at the annunciation. This is the moment when God waits for a human being to cooperate with his saving grace, on which the future of the whole world depends:

> Adam and all his poor children, exiled in the region of the shadow of death, are waiting for your response. Abraham and David are waiting. The whole world is waiting… for on your lips depends the consolation of the afflicted, the ransom of captives, the liberation of the condemned, in short, the salvation of all the children of Adam, of your whole race.[5]

The whole world, including the patriarchs, prophets and all humanity, is holding its breath, awaiting the decision of Mary as the representative of all human beings in their capacity to say yes to God. There is even cosmic importance to this moment, since heaven, earth and even the angel wait in suspense for Mary's acceptance: 'Let it be to me according to your word' (Luke 1:38).

This passage beautifully portrays Mary's (and therefore the whole of humanity's) free will in salvation history, emphasising that God waits for human cooperation, rather than forcing salvation on us, and highlights the annunciation as the turning point of history, when God's plan for redemption is set in motion. Mary can help Christians find a way to draw closer to Jesus and to one another. Twenty-first century women and men can find in her the inspiration for what it means to be a human being filled with grace, body and soul. In John's gospel she stands by her son at the foot of the cross. The beloved disciple, a model for all the followers of Christ, is told by the dying Jesus to cherish Mary as his mother, and she is told to care for him as her son. When the church is born by the power of the Holy Spirit at Pentecost, Mary is there, at the heart of the community of those who worship Jesus.

Her questions are our questions – how is it that God can work through such weak instruments as we feel ourselves to be? How can the tasteless water of our lives be turned into the life-giving wine of God's grace? Her song can also be our song, exulting in a God who enters fully into all that is fragile and earthy in human experience, into the blood and guts of human bodies but also into their beauty and their capacity to give and receive love. Like Mary, we are invited to treasure all that we know of Jesus and ponder it in our hearts. We become blessed not when, by some accident of birth, we are members of the church, but when we have made the journey of faith and learned to hear the word of God and keep it.

-

REFLECTION

- What do the key teachings about Mary outlined above tell you about your own role as a disciple of Jesus?
- Reading Luke's account of the annunciation, what do you imagine wanting to say to Mary herself and to God?

–

PRAYER

Gracious Lord Jesus, from your cross you committed your mother and beloved disciple to each other, thus creating a new family. Help all your disciples to see that we, too, are members of a family of renewed relationships, tied not by blood, but by the waters of baptism. Help us, like Mary, to treasure all your words and to ponder them in our heart. Amen.

Creation set free

9 December

Isaiah 11:1–3, 6–9

There shall come forth a shoot from the stump of Jesse,
    and a branch shall grow out of his roots.
And the Spirit of the Lord shall rest upon him,
    the spirit of wisdom and understanding,
    the spirit of counsel and might,
    the spirit of knowledge and the fear of the Lord.
And his delight shall be in the fear of the Lord…

The wolf shall dwell with the lamb,
    and the leopard shall lie down with the kid,
and the calf and the lion and the fatling together,
    and a little child shall lead them.
The cow and the bear shall feed;
    their young shall lie down together;
    and the lion shall eat straw like the ox.
The sucking child shall play over the hole of the asp,
    and the weaned child shall put his hand on the adder's den.
They shall not hurt or destroy
    in all my holy mountain;
for the earth shall be full of the knowledge of the Lord
    as the waters cover the sea.

James Cameron's 2009 film *Avatar* is a cautionary tale of science fiction which bears striking similarity to the prophecy in Isaiah 11:1–10 in its shared vision of a righteous ruler bringing peace to creation and restoring harmony between humanity and the rest of the natural world. The film presents a stark contrast between two opposing groups: the

Na'vi, indigenous dwellers of the planet Pandora, who have a deep spiritual and symbiotic connection with nature, and the human invaders of the planet, a megacorporation called the Resources Development Administration (RDA).

The Na'vi embody a holistic, reverent relationship with nature, believing that all life is connected through Eywa, their spiritual deity, who acts as a guiding, life-sustaining force. Their sacred site is the 'Tree of Souls' which is a biological network linking them to Eywa and to their ancestors. They have a bonding ritual in which they connect to animals and plants through braid-like tendrils called neural queues. This ritual symbolises unity and respect for life and can bring healing and life back to the wounded and dying.

The Na'vi see Pandora as a living being, not a resource to exploit. They live in balance with their environment, only taking what they need and honouring the life they consume. Their hunting rituals reflect a deep respect for the creatures they kill, which they thank for their sacrifice. In this they mirror the indigenous gratitude rituals of our own planet, such as those of Inuit and other Arctic groups, who believe that animals give themselves willingly to respectful hunters. Many Native American tribes also believe that animals have souls or spirits and must be respected, using every part of the animal to honour its gift of life and speaking to a hunted animal's spirit before and after a kill, thanking it for providing food and offering tobacco or painting their faces in mourning to show respect.

In contrast, the humans of the RDA in the film treat nature as something to be controlled, exploited and conquered. They have come to Pandora to mine an element called unobtanium, destroying Na'vi lands and exploiting the resources they find there, using military force and advanced technology to control the planet. They view Pandora's rich resources as valuable only for profit and despise the Na'vi as primitives whose connection to nature is an obstacle to economic gain, rather than a meaningful way of life. They rely on machines, weapons and technology to dominate Pandora, rather than seeking to adapt to it, still less to learn from it. There are clear parallels in the film with what is going on in our own world, where many indigenous peoples, who see creation as something to be nurtured and respected, are being exploited and even exterminated by governments or industrial corporations who see it as something to be exploited for power and profit.

In the film, a disabled military veteran, Jake Sully, makes a spiritual and emotional journey from being an exploiter, only interested in taking part in scientific experiments on Pandora to regain his lost mobility, to being a protector who gathers a rebellion against his military backers once he meets and falls in love with the Na'vi and their way of life. In answer to his hesitant prayers, Eywa fights back when attacked by the RDA, with nature and the animals making common cause with the Na'vi and the humans with whom they have bonded.

Avatar is not a Christian film, but it illustrates many themes embedded in the prophetic hopes centred on the Messianic vision of a redeemed world. It shows the redemptive power of reconnecting with nature and suggests that when we disrespect creation, we sow the seeds of our own ultimate downfall. There is also a commonality with the psalms and prophecies which feature God's wrath against human idolatries, expressed in raging seas, earthquakes and powerful natural phenomena. *Avatar* warns against the dangers of greed, environmental destruction and cultural arrogance.

Isaiah 11 is understood by Christians as a prophecy about Jesus Christ, speaking of a future ruler from the Davidic line who will bring justice, wisdom and harmony to the whole of creation. The apostle Paul in his letter to the Romans tells us that this is the victory won by the death and resurrection of Jesus:

> For the creation was subjected to futility, not of its own will but by the will of him who subjected it in hope; because the creation itself will be set free from its bondage to decay and obtain the glorious liberty of the children of God.
> ROMANS 8:20–21

The prophecy describes a peaceful world where natural enemies live in harmony free from violence and destruction, whose ruler, the Messiah, will judge fairly, defend the oppressed and renew creation, not by military conquest, but through wisdom and justice. Jesus' disciples watched in awe as he commanded the storm and the waves to be still, asking 'Who then is this, that even wind and sea obey him?' (Mark 4:41). Jesus as the Messiah showed that he is Lord of creation, since 'he was in the beginning with God; all things were made through him, and without him was not anything made that was made' (John 1:2–3).

Genesis 2:8–15 describes Eden as a paradise, where humans, animals and nature exist in perfect balance and unity with God, although humans are described as being given dominion over creation. This is problematic for many non-believers and also a good many Christians. In 1967, scientist Lynn White Jr. published a groundbreaking article entitled 'The historical roots of our ecological crisis' in the journal *Science*, claiming that Western Christianity, particularly in its interpretation of Genesis, was responsible for the domination and exploitation of nature. Pointing to Genesis 1:28, where God commands humans to 'subdue' the earth and 'have dominion' over all living things, he argued that this anthropocentric worldview had led to the environmental destruction seen in the Industrial Revolution and beyond, stating, 'Christianity bears a huge burden of guilt for environmental destruction.' Nevertheless, at the same time as condemning the Christian tradition for being the originator of the problem, White also saw it as potentially part of the solution if it recovered a theology of stewardship. He praised St Francis of Assisi as a model for a more ecologically friendly Christianity, calling him a 'patron saint for ecologists'.[6]

His article sparked a wide-ranging debate within and between theology, environmental ethics and ecological movements. It inspired Christian theologians to reinterpret Genesis to emphasise care rather than domination of creation and influenced later Catholic teachings, such as the late Pope Francis' encyclical *Laudato Si'* (2015), which stresses environmental responsibility. Francis claims that the earth is God's creation, and we are called to respect it. It is also in crisis through climate change, deforestation and pollution which threatens both nature and the poor. He sees everything as connected: environmental damage worsens social inequality, hitting the poor hardest. He offers a strong critique of consumerism, condemning 'throwaway culture' and reckless consumption and launches a call to action, urging governments, businesses and individuals to work together to heal the planet. All of this picks up Isaiah's vision of a world renewed through the coming of the Messiah. Whether in scientific research, science fiction or biblical teaching, the message is the same.

-

REFLECTION

- How do you respond to the issues raised in the film *Avatar*, which echo elements within Isaiah's prophecy of the Messianic age and the encyclical *Laudato Si*? Do you see them as being part of our understanding of the coming of Christ at Christmas?
- Take some time to connect with nature in any way that you can. What does this experience make you want to say to God?

-

PRAYER

God our loving Father, you are Lord of creation and through your Son Jesus Christ all things – the cosmos, the planets and our Mother Earth with all she contains – came into being. Help us to be partners with you in creation, loving and reverencing you through our love and reverence for our beautiful world. Help us to be responsible and respectful stewards of creation. Amen.

The revolution of tenderness

10 December

Isaiah 61:1–3

The Spirit of the Lord God is upon me,
*   because the Lord has anointed me*
to bring good tidings to the afflicted;
*   he has sent me to bind up the brokenhearted,*
to proclaim liberty to the captives,
*   and the opening of the prison to those who are bound;*
to proclaim the year of the Lord's favour,
*   and the day of vengeance of our God;*
*   to comfort all who mourn;*
to grant to those who mourn in Zion –
*   to give them a garland instead of ashes,*
the oil of gladness instead of mourning,
*   the mantle of praise instead of a faint spirit;*
that they may be called oaks of righteousness,
*   the planting of the Lord, that he may be glorified.*

In general, I find the shopping frenzy of Christmas too overwhelming to enjoy. There are too many things I don't want for me to decide easily what I do want, and the proliferation of sizes and colours and makes and models and general stuff just makes me want to run away and hide. Going into a large department store is like entering Aladdin's cave in terms of an immediate assault on the senses from the sight and sound and smell and feel of so much that is shiny and scented and new. Coming out into the ordinary world afterwards, there can be quite a contrast between the world inside, where everything is designed to attract and charm the shopper, and the world outside, where we generally have to make do with what things really look like, whether attractive or not.

Both as canny shoppers and as people living in the real world, we have to discern where real beauty lies and look beneath the surface of things to find their true value. It's also part of the prophecy of Isaiah, which Jesus proclaimed about himself in the synagogue in Nazareth (Luke 4:16–21), that an integral part of the Messiah's calling (and therefore of the calling of all who follow Jesus the Messiah), is to bring good tidings to the afflicted and to bind up the broken-hearted. We can't do this at second hand, watching the afflicted and the broken-hearted from a safe and sanitised distance. Pope Francis repeatedly said and wrote that the church isn't meant to be a powerful institution but a field hospital for the wounded, meeting people where they are. In his exhortation *The Joy of the Gospel* he stated:

> Jesus washed the feet of his disciples. The Lord gets involved and he involves his own, as he kneels to wash their feet. He tells his disciples: 'You will be blessed if you do this' (John 13:17). An evangelizing community gets involved by word and deed in people's daily lives; it bridges distances, it is willing to abase itself if necessary, and it embraces human life, touching the suffering flesh of Christ in others. Evangelizers thus take on the 'smell of the sheep' and the sheep are willing to hear their voice. An evangelizing community is also supportive, standing by people at every step of the way, no matter how difficult or lengthy this may prove to be.[7]

The 'sheep' may be very smelly indeed, but it doesn't work to hold our noses at a distance, we need to get down and dirty where Jesus is sleeping in our shop doorways, begging in our streets and sitting in a drunken or drug-induced haze, feeling overwhelmed by isolation and despair. Coming out of a store in London's busiest shopping area some years ago in the run-up to Christmas, I went through a door into a quiet back street. All of a sudden, I was out of the world of sparkling Christmas lights, carols blaring and food shops selling Christmas goodies into a colder, darker side of the city. I almost tripped over a homeless man, wrapped up against the cold, who lay asleep in the shop doorway with his back to the passers-by. It was a glaring contrast with all the glitz and gaudiness of the shop windows. He looked lonely and vulnerable, down on the cold ground, scarcely distinguishable from the black bin bags of evil-smelling rubbish that lay piled up beside him. I went through all the questions that must go through most people's heads at such a moment: is he still alive, should I try to wake him up and offer help and comfort, what if he doesn't want to be woken up and gets angry with me for interfering, what if, what if…?

The UK homelessness charity Shelter reports that on any given night in 2024, there were over 354,000 people who were homeless, which is 1 in 160 people, with that statistic rising to 1 in 47 people in London. They report that 'homelessness in England is at a record high and is continuing to rise. Across the country expensive, damp, crumbling homes are making people sick and holding them back.'[8] Not every homeless person is on the streets, and many children are currently living in housing that is totally unfit, barely better than the cold, smelly stable in Bethlehem, filled with animals and open to strangers.

It's not always easy to know what to do or say when faced with the lived reality of such desperation, but any study of homelessness I've read from those with more experience and expertise than mine says that above all people on the streets want to be looked at and treated as if they are someone, as if they matter. Standing on that London pavement, looking at the man asleep in the doorway, I found myself thinking that if Christmas is about light and beauty, glory and giving, it's also about poverty and vulnerability, about the littleness and homelessness of God, who had nowhere to shelter. Fred Pratt Green's Advent hymn 'Long ago, prophets knew' asks a hard question: when Jesus comes, will he be welcome? Jesus comes into our world and stands before us in many guises. What kind of a welcome can he expect from us? Again, in *The Joy of the Gospel*, Pope Francis called for Christians to prioritise mercy over judgement, closeness over distance and tenderness over coldness:

> Many try to escape from others and take refuge in the comfort of their privacy or in a small circle of close friends, renouncing

the realism of the social aspect of the Gospel. For just as some people want a purely spiritual Christ, without flesh and without the cross, they also want their interpersonal relationships provided by sophisticated equipment, by screens and systems which can be turned on and off on command. Meanwhile, the Gospel tells us constantly to run the risk of a face-to-face encounter with others, with their physical presence which challenges us, with their pain and their pleas, with their joy which infects us in our close and continuous interaction. True faith in the incarnate Son of God is inseparable from self-giving, from membership in the community, from service, from reconciliation with others. The Son of God, by becoming flesh, summoned us to the revolution of tenderness.[9]

What would it be like, all over the world this Advent, if Christians responded to that call to become revolutionaries?

–

REFLECTION

- How do you respond to the idea of becoming a 'revolutionary of tenderness'? What difference might that make to yourself and to others?
- Spend some time in your imagination with Joseph, knocking on doors with his wife going into labour and repeatedly being turned away. What would you want to do for them?

–

PRAYER

Lord Jesus, you came into our world as a stranger, without home or shelter. Give us open hearts and creative minds to respond to the problems of our times, learning in your name to become revolutionaries of tenderness. Amen.

Prince of Peace

11 December

Isaiah 2:1–5

The word which Isaiah the son of Amoz saw concerning Judah and Jerusalem.

> *It shall come to pass in the latter days*
> *that the mountain of the house of the Lord*
> *shall be established as the highest of the mountains,*
> *and shall be raised above the hills;*
> *and all the nations shall flow to it,*
> *and many peoples shall come, and say:*
> *'Come, let us go up to the mountain of the Lord,*
> *to the house of the God of Jacob;*
> *that he may teach us his ways*
> *and that we may walk in his paths.'*
> *For out of Zion shall go forth the law,*
> *and the word of the Lord from Jerusalem.*
> *He shall judge between the nations,*
> *and shall decide for many peoples;*
> *and they shall beat their swords into ploughshares,*
> *and their spears into pruning hooks;*
> *nation shall not lift up sword against nation,*
> *neither shall they learn war anymore.*
> *O house of Jacob,*
> *come, let us walk*
> *in the light of the Lord.*

The traditional African American spiritual 'Down by the riverside' dates back to before the American Civil War and is believed to have originated among enslaved people in the southern United States.

The song speaks of laying down one's sword and shield 'down by the riverside' and choosing a path of peace instead of war in the repeated refrain, 'Ain't gonna study war no more.' The song has clear references to today's prophecy from Isaiah and emphasises a commitment to non-violence by turning away from conflict.

The song, with its repetition of the 'riverside', is thought to symbolise baptism and the rituals of water associated with cleansing, salvation and rebirth in the Christian tradition. At the same time scholars suggest that the references to crossing a river could be connected with the Ohio River, which separated slave states from free states during the Civil War or with the Underground Railroad via which many runaway slaves escaped to freedom.

Whatever the original meaning of the song, it became popular during the Civil Rights Movement of the 1950s and 60s and later during the Vietnam War and other wars as a protest song, reinforcing the themes of non-violence, freedom and social justice. It was widely recorded by artists including Louis Armstrong, Pete Seeger and Mahalia Jackson and remains a staple in gospel music, but it is also performed in folk, blues and jazz styles.

'Down by the riverside' is not a common Advent or Christmas song, but the theme of peace and peace-making is dominant in many of the Advent readings. Although in a completely different musical style, one of the most famous sections of Handel's *Messiah* is the chorus 'For unto us a child is born', which declares Jesus to be the Messiah promised by Isaiah:

> For unto us a child is born, unto us a son is given: and the government shall be upon his shoulder: and his name shall be called Wonderful, Counsellor, The mighty God, The everlasting Father, The Prince of Peace.
>
> ISAIAH 9:6 (KJV)

There's a particular challenge in praying with this and similar texts from the Hebrew scriptures at a time when the Holy Land is in the midst of a devastating conflict between peoples and faiths with rival claims to divine revelation and to the land itself. We have a ringing prophecy of peace and non-violence emanating precisely from the violently contested city of Jerusalem in the equally contested land of Judah. Yet if the mountain of the house of the Lord is to be 'established as the highest of the mountains' this is clearly not, either in Isaiah's Messianic vision or in the teachings of Jesus, because one people or faith community has managed to lay definitive and exclusive claim to it.

Isaiah makes clear, and Jesus takes up this prophecy, that all the nations, not just one, will go up to the mountain of the Lord, so that the God of Jacob can teach the whole world his ways and show the entire human family how to walk in his paths. The gospels show us that Jesus himself had to learn this, and he learned it precisely from his encounters with pagans whom his own people saw as distinctly 'other'.

We have the rather startling story of his encounter with the Syro-Phoenician woman in Mark 7:24–30. She accosts him to ask his help with her sick daughter, who is possessed by a demon. Jesus responds in a way that strikes many people as distinctly unsympathetic if not downright rude: 'Let the children first be fed, for it is not right to take the children's bread and throw it to the dogs' (v. 27). He is the Messiah of the Jews and has come principally to save the Jews. But the woman won't take no for an answer. The mother's distress makes her determined to press her case and she argues straight back, 'Yes, Lord; yet even the dogs under the table eat the children's crumbs.' He is struck by her faith and her love-driven boldness and grants her the miracle she so desperately wants.

In this story we see Jesus being open to persuasion and to having his views changed by his encounter with a woman (one problem for a Jewish man) from an alien people (yet another problem). This doesn't mean that we use prayer to wheedle our way into God's good graces in order to get whatever we want, but it does remind us that in his humanity Jesus was as open to change, to being taken by surprise and to learning as we all are.

Perhaps this surprise and the openness to the salvation of non-Jews that it brought about lies beneath another encounter, this time with an outright enemy, a member of the occupying Roman army. In Luke's account the local Jewish elders plead on the centurion's behalf. He has clearly integrated into the local community to an extent, since they tell Jesus that he is a man who loves their nation and has built the local synagogue for them. When the centurion shows humility and cultural sensitivity as well as faith, assuring Jesus that he need not render himself unclean by entering a pagan house, Jesus is amazed, remarking, 'I tell you, not even in Israel have I found such faith' (Luke 7:9).

If Jesus is the God of surprises, then he is also open to being surprised by unlooked-for faith, and himself experiences faith as a continuous journey. This is true not only for us as individuals but for the faith community as a whole. These gospel stories sow the seeds of the major shift that we see in the early church when Jesus' Jewish disciples learn that salvation is for anyone who is faithful and courageous enough to ask for it. Such shifts of emphasis and perspective have happened repeatedly in Christian history. They aren't always comfortable or easy, but they are a sign that our faith remains alive.

What do these stories and readings say to us, as we embark on the journey to Bethlehem? Isaiah was prophesying at a time of considerable religious and cultural threat. The Assyrian Empire was the dominant superpower of the time and was expanding aggressively, dragging the kingdoms of Israel and Judah into conflicts between Assyria and smaller regional powers. Judah became a vassal state of Assyria while the Assyrians destroyed the kingdom of Israel and took many Israelites into exile. It was a time of political instability and spiritual and social decline into idolatry, oppression of the poor, corruption and moral decay. It all sounds strangely familiar. Our newspapers and the internet repeatedly tell us that the global landscape is shifting, and that old alliances and securities are disintegrating. We look to an uncertain economic and political future and global climate change looms like a dark cloud over our own and our children's future. Borders are threatened by conquest and by mass migration driven by war and economic instability. Yet here is Isaiah proclaiming the coming of the Messiah as Prince of Peace. He promises a God whose desire is to teach us to walk and live in his ways. However uncertain we may feel, that choice is ours.

-

REFLECTION

- How have you experienced praying with this text in light of current world conflicts?
- How do you respond to the invitation to turn away from conflict both as a citizen of your country and as an individual person?
- What might it be like for you to 'walk in the light of the Lord'?

-

PRAYER

Lord Jesus, you are the Prince of Peace. Bring peace to our troubled times, and make each one of us an instrument of peace in our world and among our families, colleagues and friends. Amen.

Loving our enemies

12 December

Luke 6:27–38

'But I say to you that hear, Love your enemies, do good to those who hate you, bless those who curse you, pray for those who abuse you. To him who strikes you on the cheek, offer the other also; and from him who takes away your coat do not withhold even your shirt. Give to every one who begs from you; and of him who takes away your goods do not ask them again. And as you wish that men would do to you, do so to them.

'If you love those who love you, what credit is that to you? For even sinners love those who love them. And if you do good to those who do good to you, what credit is that to you? For even sinners do the same. And if you lend to those from whom you hope to receive, what credit is that to you? Even sinners lend to sinners, to receive as much again. But love your enemies, and do good, and lend, expecting nothing in return; and your reward will be great, and you will be sons of the Most High; for he is kind to the ungrateful and the selfish. Be merciful, even as your Father is merciful.

'Judge not, and you will not be judged; condemn not, and you will not be condemned; forgive, and you will be forgiven; give, and it will be given to you; good measure, pressed down, shaken together, running over, will be put into your lap. For the measure you give will be the measure you get back.'

Bert, a boyhood friend of my father's, knew a lot about God's mercy. He was captured by the Japanese during World War II and imprisoned in one of the notorious death camps on the Burma Railway. Also known as the Death Railway, it was a 258-mile railway built by Japan to support its military operations in Burma (now Myanmar). It connected Bangkok in

Thailand to Rangoon in Burma and was constructed between 1942 and 1943 by over 60,000 Allied prisoners of war alongside around 250,000 workers from Asia, mainly Burmese, Thai, Malay and Indonesian. All the workers endured horrific starvation, disease, brutal beatings and overwork. They were subjected to torture and executions for failing to meet work quotas, and over 100,000 of them died from disease and exhaustion. After Japan's defeat, the railway was mostly abandoned, though some sections are still in use today, and war-crime trials were held for Japanese officers involved in the railway's construction. The railway itself remains a symbol of suffering and resilience, with memorials in Thailand and Myanmar.

One of the most remarkable yet lesser-known acts of resilience during the horrors of the Burma Railway was the creation of an art exhibition in Chungkai Camp. Organised by British prisoners of war, including cartoonist Ronald Searle, it showcased drawings, paintings and crafts made under brutal conditions. As well as documenting the suffering of the prisoners and the sadistic violence of their guards, the exhibition served as a rare escape from the horrors of war as well as an outlet for the prisoners seeking solace in creativity and self-expression. Many of the artworks reflected Christian faith, showing prayers, biblical scenes and Christ-like endurance in the face of suffering. Some prisoners found strength in their faith, believing that beauty and creativity were acts of defiance against despair. One man depicted Christ crucified, using only driftwood and nails, and slowly this particular exhibit began to draw the prisoners to prayer and pilgrimage. They would come to stand in front of it, gaining strength and comfort at the thought of Jesus willingly taking on being humiliated and mistreated as they were, for love of all humankind.

One day, feeling particularly low, Bert had taken refuge in the art hut to pray before the suffering Christ, when to his horror he heard the familiar boots of a camp guard approaching. Bert stood rigidly to attention, expecting a savage beating from the butt of the guard's rifle at any moment, but instead the guard stood beside him and quietly began to weep. When Bert dared to turn his head to look at his neighbour, the soldier whispered, 'I, too, am a Christian.' The two men saluted one another, and the guard turned on his heel and walked away. Bert told me this story years later, remembering it as a moment in his life when he saw a glimpse of repentance on the face of one whom he judged as a merciless enemy. In that moment he himself was called upon to have mercy. It began for both of them by being able to recognise and acknowledge the humanity in the other before their mutual Saviour.

There were other stories of Christian witness and forgiveness from the Burma Railway, despite the unimaginable suffering. Ernest Gordon, a Scottish Army officer whose story inspired the book and film *To End All Wars*, was near death from fever and starvation, but was cared for by fellow prisoners who encouraged him with their Christian faith. After the war, Gordon forgave his captors and became a Christian minister, preaching about faith, suffering and reconciliation. British officer Eric Lomax was subjected to prolonged and severe torture by his Japanese interrogator, Nagase Takashi. Lomax subsequently suffered years of trauma and hatred, but would discover, years later, that his former tor-turer had become a man of peace, deeply regretting his past. Instead of seeking revenge, Lomax met with him in Thailand in 1993 and forgave him. The two men became close friends until Lomax's death in 2012. His memoir, *The Railway Man*, was later adapted into a film which tells this remarkable story.

Learning to forgive or even tolerate an enemy in conditions as appall-ingly cruel and inhumane as the Burma Railway death camps seems impossible to imagine. The prisoners of war in Japan or Europe that I have met never denied the evil that had been done to them. But several of them were remarkable for their deep understanding of and openness to other human beings. It was as if they had seen the worst that people can do to one another, and in doing so had discovered their own deepest capacity for sympathy and understanding. The let-ter of James speaks of peacemakers sowing in peace and reaping a harvest of righteousness (James 3:18). That is not the result of weak or passive virtue, but of the strength that lies within mercy and is the fruit of extraordinary resilience and compassion.

There is a medieval mystical text, written by an anonymous author, called *The Cloud of Unknowing*. In its final chapter the author writes: 'It is not what you are nor what you have been that God looks at with his merciful eyes, but what you desire to be.'[10] Our news media and the blogosphere are full of people making harsh judgements of one another, but most of us reserve our harshest criticism for ourselves. If you ask a group of people to write down six positive things about themselves and six negative things, it's remarkable how quickly they fill up the negative column but seem to struggle to fill the positive one. We can be our own worst enemy and harshest judge in this respect.

The Cloud of Unknowing presents a different picture in talking about God's judgement. For God, human life is not a performance-related activity, to be judged on output or impact. God knows what we are and what we have been, but looks beyond our achievements, to our deepest desires. In that secret place of our innermost heart, where we long to be good, however much our behaviour may betray that longing, God's merciful eyes see and understand our need of grace. It is a similar understanding of this compassion of God that Muslims remember in the *Basmalah*, the phrase 'In the name of God, the compassionate, the merciful', which begins each chapter of the Qur'an. This prayer is used habitually as the opening of each action, in order to receive a blessing from God.

It is this compassion of God that Jesus called on from the cross when he said, 'Father, forgive them; for they know not what they do' (Luke 23:34). In the moment in the Burmese camp, it was not the Japanese tyrant and Bert, the British victim, who stood side by side before the cross of Christ. It was two human beings who recognised each other as fellow sinners whose deepest need was for God's mercy. Perhaps that moment was the beginning of reconciliation.

–

REFLECTION

- How do you understand forgiveness and reconciliation?
- Have you ever felt the need to forgive or to be forgiven? How have you experienced God in that situation or in situations such as those on the Burma Railway and elsewhere that you know about?

–

PRAYER

Lord Jesus, you had mercy on those who put you to death and prayed with compassion that they might be forgiven. Help us to look on one another's failings with mercy and understanding, so that we can become instruments of your peace. Amen.

Teacher of wisdom

13 December

Isaiah 30: 19–21, 23–26

Yea, O people in Zion who dwell at Jerusalem; you shall weep no more. He will surely be gracious to you at the sound of your cry; when he hears it, he will answer you. And though the Lord give you the bread of adversity and the water of affliction, yet your Teacher will not hide himself any more, but your eyes shall see your Teacher. And your ears shall hear a word behind you, saying, 'This is the way, walk in it,' when you turn to the right or when you turn to the left…

And he will give rain for the seed with which you sow the ground, and grain, the produce of the ground, which will be rich and plenteous. In that day your cattle will graze in large pastures; and the oxen and the asses that till the ground will eat salted provender, which has been winnowed with shovel and fork. And upon every lofty mountain and every high hill there will be brooks running with water, in the day of the great slaughter, when the towers fall. Moreover the light of the moon will be as the light of the sun, and the light of the sun will be sevenfold, as the light of seven days, in the day when the Lord binds up the hurt of his people, and heals the wounds inflicted by his blow.

Did you have a favourite teacher at school? I was immensely blessed to have two wonderful English teachers. At primary school we would be taken outside to observe nature or just run around and hear our feet crunching through the autumn leaves or splashing in the puddles. We would run our hands through water or listen to birdsong and then were told to sit down immediately and write about what we saw and heard and felt. We had stories read to us with all the different voices, so that characters came to life and swept us up in their tale. To this day Toad, Ratty and Mole in *The Wind in the Willows* still speak to me in those voices, all belonging to the one teacher.

Our secondary school English teacher had a wonderful speaking voice and could silence a room of lively pupils by reading Shakespeare or poetry. She also taught Latin with unsurpassed brilliance, holding our attention with funny rhymes to help us remember grammatical rules and even managing to make past participles and ablative absolutes fun. In later years she ditched the English exam syllabus for two weeks and taught us Anglo-Saxon poetry, just for our education and enjoyment. I still have a taste for its haunting rhythms.

Our otherwise strict and sometimes terrifying geography teacher read *The Lord of the Rings* during handwriting classes, and no Aragorn has ever been more majestic, no Gollum more hissingly sinister. She clearly loved it, and so did we.

The sign of a good teacher, in my experience, is someone who can hold your attention and build up your confidence in your own abilities, however meagre they may be or challenging the task before you. They can communicate, even to reluctant learners, their own love of the subject and their sense of it being exciting and worthwhile to work at it.

So what does it mean for God to be called our teacher, and what are we learning? The Advent hymn 'O come, O come Emmanuel' addresses Jesus as divine Wisdom:

> *O come, Thou Wisdom from on high,*
> *Who orders all things mightily;*
> *To us the path of knowledge show,*
> *And cause us in her ways to go.*

But what wisdom and knowledge do we learn from God? The Christmas story itself points to the contrast between God's wisdom and that of the world. No one wanting to convince everyone of a message would begin with the wordlessness of a tiny baby who would live and grow in obscurity for some 30 years before preaching it to a ragtag crowd of fishermen, prostitutes and undesirables while the educated and powerful listened in contemptuous disbelief. Paul tells us:

> For the foolishness of God is wiser than men, and the weakness of God is stronger than men. For consider your call, brethren; not many of you were wise according to worldly standards, not many were powerful, not many were of noble birth; but God chose what is foolish in the world to shame the wise, God chose what is weak in the world to shame the strong, God chose what is low and despised in the world, even things that are not, to bring to nothing things that are, so that no human being might boast in the presence of God. He is the source of your life in Christ Jesus, whom God made our wisdom, our righteousness and sanctification and redemption.
> 1 CORINTHIANS 1:25–30

If the God of Advent and Christmas is our teacher, then we are being taught a wisdom completely unlike that of a world organised according to the rule of the jungle, in which might is right, the fittest survive by treading on the vulnerable, and the prevailing wisdom is 'everyone for themself'. The nineteenth-century carol 'See amid the winter's snow' by Edward Caswall has a verse:

> *Teach, O teach us, Holy Child,*
> *By Thy face so meek and mild,*
> *Teach us to resemble Thee,*
> *In Thy sweet humility.*

How are we to learn the humility of the Christ-child? One of the most villainous figures in literary history is Uriah Heep from Charles Dickens' *David Copperfield*. He constantly stresses his humility and his respect for his employers, but all the while he is seething with envy and thwarted ambition, and scheming for the downfall of those whose better fortune he hates and resents.

This is not the humility we find in the scriptures. In the book of Numbers, God says of Moses: 'He is faithful in all my house. With him I speak face to face' (Numbers 12:7–8, NRSV). Yet it's also said of this unique man, who has seen God's face and lived, that he is the humblest man on earth (Numbers 12:3). Moses knows his own weakness, begging God to give the burden of leadership to someone else, as he is such a poor speaker (Exodus 4:13). God still chooses Moses, despite his limitations, but also sends his brother Aaron, who is far more eloquent. Moses has a very direct relationship with God, saying exactly what he thinks and feels. Perhaps this is the meaning of being at home in God's house. Moses doesn't spend his time being on his best behaviour and minding his Ps and Qs.

Closeness to God and humility appear to go hand in hand. If we only know our own poverty to deplore and try to hide it, then it does us no good at all. If we know it and, as a result, are amazed by the lavishness of God's gifts to us, then it gives us a sense of how blessed we are to have received graces that we did nothing to earn or deserve.

St Ignatius tells us that humility is not the same as self-abasement. To make self-belittling comments about or to ourselves is not humility but ingratitude for God's gifts. When we come across someone with a high opinion of themselves, we try to cut them down to size, asking, 'Who does she think she is – God's gift?' The correct answer is yes, we are, each and every one of us, God's gift to the world.

But this is a cause for humble gratitude rather than for self-aggrandisement. Gratitude is at the heart of true humility, for it is our appreciative response for God's gifts given freely to one who didn't earn or deserve them. This leads us to turn in wonder and loving thanks to the giver of the gift. A person who becomes able to thank God daily for every gift, however small, becomes increasingly aware of the endless, often barely visible signs of God's loving, grace-giving presence at every moment. We may be fully aware of our limitations, but we become even more fully aware of the extent of God's mercy, 'new every morning' (Lamentations 3:22–23).

The gratitude that brims over from knowing this is expressed in a humility that focuses on God's compassion and amazing grace rather than on our failures to measure up to our own exalted standards. That is what divine Wisdom, born in a stable, placed in a cattle trough and worshipped by shepherds teaches us.

-

REFLECTION

- What have you learned about God from a wise teacher, or directly from God? How has that affected your life, and how would you put it into words for someone else?
- What gifts has God given you that you are grateful for today?

-

PRAYER

Jesus, child in the manger, who chose to reveal yourself to the humble and the outcast, show us the humble path of true knowledge and teach us to know and recognise your gifts within us, around us and in the everyday. Amen.

Higher power   14 December

Luke 21:25–36

'And there will be signs in sun and moon and stars, and upon the
earth distress of nations in perplexity at the roaring of the sea and
the waves, men fainting with fear and with foreboding of what is
coming on the world; for the powers of the heavens will be shaken.
And then they will see the Son of man coming in a cloud with power
and great glory. Now when these things begin to take place, look
up and raise your heads, because your redemption is drawing near.'

And he told them a parable: 'Look at the fig tree, and all the
trees; as soon as they come out in leaf, you see for yourselves and
know that the summer is already near. So also, when you see
these things taking place, you know that the kingdom of God is
near. Truly, I say to you, this generation will not pass away till all
has taken place. Heaven and earth will pass away, but my words
will not pass away.

But take heed to yourselves lest your hearts be weighed down
with dissipation and drunkenness and cares of this life, and that
day come upon you suddenly like a snare; for it will come upon
all who dwell upon the face of the whole earth. But watch at all
times, praying that you may have strength to escape all these
things that will take place, and to stand before the Son of man.'

I think of myself as someone who has very little self-control. However
good my New Year's resolutions, they're nearly always broken by
mid-January. However much I may tell myself that I really don't need
any chocolate right now, someone only has to wave a wrapper in my
direction, and I've fallen off the wagon. Anyone working in the field of
helping people to break bad habits knows that self-control is basically
about desire. We need to desire the goal we're aiming for more than
the bad habit we're trying to break. That desire can keep us going,

even when the temptation to give up and give in is almost overwhelming. It's also about recognising our own weakness and our need for help from what, in addiction circles, is called the 'Higher Power'. For Christians, the 'Higher Power' is God, who knows our weakness, and willingly enters into it to share his power and help us to overcome it.

The medieval anchoress Julian of Norwich wrote *Revelations of Divine Love* (known in an earlier version as *Showings*) some time after she experienced a series of visions in May 1373. The era in which she lived spanned both the Black Death and the Peasants' Revolt of 1381 as well as the widespread unrest caused within church and society by the Lollards and the Great Schism within the Western Church, so hers was certainly not a life of peaceful safety away from the troubles of the world. Julian received a vivid series of insights into God's meaning in creating and saving the world and shared her personal experience so as to help her fellow Christians find the same reassurance in a dark world, and find a union with God that would help to free them from whatever held them captive in toxic or damaging habits and behaviour.

In chapter 51 of *Revelations of Divine Love*, we find an extended parable of the lord and the servant, in which Julian conflates a number of scriptural images and the story of salvation. She is deeply troubled by the whole question of sin and the damage that it does to us and to our world. God has told her that 'all shall be well' but, like many of us, she looks at the mess the world is in and the effects of sin and asks how all can possibly be well, given the state of things. She finds an answer in the person of Jesus, who is both the second person of the Trinity and the 'second Adam' and comes into the world to share the whole of our human condition and redeem it from within.

She reflects on the fall of Adam, using the image of a servant who is devoted to his master's service and goes rushing off to do his bidding, only to fall down into a pit and to lie there in the darkness, bruised and battered, bemoaning his fate and unable to get up out of the pit without help. The servant's fall represents humanity's fall into sin and suffering. Instead of looking up to his lord and trusting in his power to help him, the servant is overwhelmed by his pain and failure, symbolising how sin and suffering can cloud our view of God's mercy. The lord doesn't become angry but looks at the servant with compassion. At the same time the servant also represents Jesus, who humbles himself by emptying himself of power and 'falling' into the human condition, including the suffering and death that are part of our human lot, to redeem humanity from within that powerless condition. As Paul says:

> In Christ God was reconciling the world to himself, not counting their trespasses against them... For our sake he made the one who knew no sin to be sin, so that in him we might become the righteousness of God.
> 2 CORINTHIANS 5:19, 21 (NRSV)

Julian's vision firmly rejects the idea of an angry, punishing God. Instead, she sees that even when we fall, God's response is love, not wrath. Like the father in Jesus' parable of the prodigal son (Luke 15:11–32), God rejoices when we hold out our need of his generous compassion, and rushes to meet us halfway on our journey. Jesus voluntarily undertakes the 'fall' for our sake. Human suffering and weakness are embraced and transformed in Jesus, in whose own sufferings we find redemption and a reflection of our human condition.

Julian sees God as looking on human beings even in all their sin with love. In an unusual image, she describes Jesus as our mother who tenderly makes us aware of the fullness of God's mercy and grace through creating, redeeming and saving us. At the same time, she describes Jesus as our 'homeliest home', in whom we find the fullness of God's love. As John writes: 'No one has ever seen God; the only Son, who is in the bosom of the Father, he has made him known' (John 1:18).

Looking at Jesus' warning in the passage from Luke's gospel where we began, this is what makes it possible for us to face the parts of our life that have become out of kilter with honesty and hope. Self-control isn't just about going on a diet, giving up smoking or making lifestyle changes so that we can look and feel better. It's about facing the habits of character and of relationship out of which we live on a daily basis. Most of us don't choose deliberately to be bad-tempered, untruthful, selfish and the like. But we're faced with daily choices about how we talk and behave, how we treat others. These small, apparently trivial choices accumulate and become the shape of our character, our way of life. Jesus talks about the impossibility of getting good fruit from a bad or sterile tree (Matthew 12:33–35) and Paul reminds us that we tend to reap what we sow (Galatians 6:7). Through God's grace we can bear the good fruit we desire if we cultivate good habits day by day.

David J. Evans' hymn 'Be still for the presence of the Lord' reminds us that God's power is moving among us here and now. It says that no work is too hard for God and encourages us to receive grace in faith. Jesus encourages us to hold our heads up in faith and hope, because help is at hand. Julian of Norwich ends her book by asking what God's meaning was in showing her these visions of the redemptive suffering of Jesus. She concludes:

> So I was taught that love is our Lord's meaning and I saw very certainly in this and in everything that before God made us he loved us, which love has never abated and never will be and in this love our life is everlasting.[11]

God's love is eternal and unchanging, and it existed before creation. It is constant and never diminishes. Our salvation and eternal life and our ability to journey in faith so as to grow nearer to God are rooted in that unconditional love.

–

REFLECTION

- Spend some time thinking about habits of thinking, speaking or acting that you feel the need to change.
- Look at the parable of the prodigal son (Luke 15:11–32) or perhaps an illustration of the scene, such as Rembrandt's famous painting. What do you want to say to the loving Father who waits to welcome you home?

–

PRAYER

Loving God, your power can overcome all our weakness and the unsteadiness of our resolution. When we're unable to fight what holds us fast, set us free by your grace, and make us strong in resisting temptation. Amen.

WEEK 3

HOPE IN DARKNESS

Signs of hope 15 December

Malachi 3:1–4

> *'Behold, I send my messenger to prepare the way before me, and the Lord whom you seek will suddenly come to his temple; the messenger of the covenant in whom you delight, behold, he is coming, says the Lord of hosts. But who can endure the day of his coming, and who can stand when he appears?*
>
> *'For he is like a refiner's fire and like fullers' soap; he will sit as a refiner and purifier of silver, and he will purify the sons of Levi and refine them like gold and silver, till they present right offerings to the Lord. Then the offering of Judah and Jerusalem will be pleasing to the Lord as in the days of old and as in former years.'*

Advent is a time when the scriptures speak to us of hope – a hope that shines through the gloom of despair, cynicism and disappointment like a candle in the dark. Hope is a virtue – it's a free gift given to us by God. We don't receive it because we've worked for it or earned it, but because God loves us. Hope is also a habit – it's a way of thinking about our present reality and future prospects, and acting like people who trust in the ultimate triumph and power of God's goodness, whatever life brings. Broadcaster Krista Tippett writes:

> Hope, like every virtue, is a choice that becomes a practice that becomes spiritual muscle memory. It's a renewable resource for moving through life as it is, not as we wish it to be.[12]

Above all, hope is what lies under our prayers when we ask God to intervene in our lives or the life of the world.

Seven years ago, on a hot summer's day in the shrine of Lourdes in France, I was feeling very far from hopeful. I'd been lighting yet another candle as I prayed for my niece, who'd been trying in vain for some years to have a baby. The medical prognosis was not encouraging, and I'd lost count of the number of prayers I'd said, shrines I'd visited and bone-freezing holy wells I'd bathed in to pray for the needed miracle. I was praying in front of the shrine of Mary, the mother of Jesus, who brought an unexpected child into the world. I thought she might understand, and help. I also prayed to the Son whom she held in her arms as a baby in Bethlehem. I was full of frustration and sadness, ranting away as I poured out my heart. 'What more do you want?', I asked. 'I've prayed as hard as I know how, and nothing's happened. How difficult can it be for you to give one girl a baby that she longs for?'

I knew that I was praying in a place full of people who were desperate for a miracle for themselves or their loved ones, so why should I be singled out for special treatment when the prayers of others went unanswered? The answers to this dilemma are not clear, and there was no direct answer to my impassioned prayers, but amid the silence, I felt that I was being given the encouragement to keep on praying in hope. A week before Christmas that same year, my niece asked me if I could let up a bit on the whole lighting candles and visiting shrines thing. 'I'm expecting twins', she said, 'and I'm afraid that if you go on praying so hard it could turn out to be triplets!' She subsequently gave birth to two beautiful, healthy babies, a reminder to me never to lose hope when I pray. Of course, I was full of gratitude and delight, but whether or not we get the answer we seek, the hard questions around petitionary prayer remain the same.

In Matthew 6, Jesus gives a masterclass in prayer. He tells us, 'Your Father knows what you need before you ask him' (Matthew 6:8). Philosophers argue that God, as an all-knowing and all-loving being, knows what is truly best for us, so just as a wise parent doesn't grant every single request from a child, God may refuse certain prayers, because granting them would not ultimately lead to our good.

Critics of this view reject this depiction of God as being selective in answering prayer but respond along the lines of God's sovereignty:

prayer is not about controlling God's will but aligning with it (1 John 5:14). They also say that God set up a world with physical laws and usually does not override them arbitrarily. Also some prayers for relief from disaster or peace in the world require our cooperation, since God gives us the precious gift of free will to work with the grace and strength he gives. Miraculous answers to prayer are rare. If God regularly intervened in obvious ways, our faith would be forced and that would undermine our free will.

Prayer is not about transaction but about transforming us and bringing us into deeper communion with him. Jesus demonstrates this in the garden of Gethsemane, praying, 'Not my will but yours be done' (Luke 22:42, NRSV), and we see Mary doing this when she says yes to the angel's message at the annunciation: 'Behold, I am the handmaid of the Lord; let it be to me according to your word' (Luke 1:38). Some people view unanswered prayer as a test of faith or an opportunity to trust God's greater wisdom, citing Job, who prayed for relief from his torment but ultimately learned to trust God's wisdom (Job 42:5–6), or Paul, who prayed for his 'thorn in the flesh' to be removed but was told, 'My grace is sufficient for you' (2 Corinthians 12:9). An apparently unanswered prayer is not a punishment or getting the cold shoulder from God. Prayer is more than just a request system; it's a process involving faith, transformation and trust in God's wisdom.

Prayer isn't something we do for God; it's something God does for us. Human beings are wired for God, so when we respond to the desire to pray, that desire is in itself evidence that God's grace is already at work within us. We may not know clearly what it is that we really, really want, but God knows it, and when we pray regularly, our deepest desires and God's response to them come into focus. The answer to the question 'When should we pray?' is – all day long. But that doesn't mean abandoning real life and forcing ourselves to think pious thoughts all the time. Whenever we're conscious of gift and blessing – in the natural world around us, in our own skills and capacities, the companionship of friends and family, the overcoming of problems and difficulties, the relieving of pain and reconciling of conflict – all this is prayer. It's the stuff of daily life, moment by moment, and when we share that with God in thanksgiving, in petition or just blind clinging on in dogged hope, without any idea of what's coming next – that is prayer. Whether first thing in the morning, last thing at night or just at snatched moments during a hectic day, that resting in or reaching out for God's sustaining presence in our lives is the greatest gift we could ask for or receive, and we know that God always hears us.

The prophet Malachi offers a message of hope to people who fear that God is not listening to their prayers for deliverance. God promises to send the longed-for Messiah to a desolate people. The birth of Jesus is a sign of hope, but it's also a challenge to cooperate with him in bringing about the kingdom of God that he promises. He is born on earth so that in our turn we might bring to birth a more just and hopeful world. Hope trusts in the power of God to help us choose love, generosity and courage over cruelty, selfishness and fear. This is the hope that Jesus brings at Christmas to a world torn apart by violence and greed. Each one of us, whatever our circumstances, is called to be a messenger of hope, proclaiming a revolution of tenderness.

Our life may be difficult, and across our country and our world we see many people struggling. But God's promises are sure, and God's love will never fail us.

–

REFLECTION

- What is your experience of prayer and of asking God for things in prayer?
- Has the discussion on prayer here raised any questions for you?
- Reading Malachi's words, what is your experience of hope and confidence in God's promises?

–

PRAYER

Loving God, you tell us that those who hope in you will renew their strength and rise on wings like eagles (Isaiah 40:31). Help us to be strong in faith, hope and love, so that we can become the embodiment of the hope you offer, messengers of your good news to a suffering world. Amen.

Daughter of Zion

16 December

Luke 1:46b–55

And Mary said,
'My soul magnifies the Lord,
and my spirit rejoices in God my Saviour,
for he has regarded the low estate of his handmaiden.
For behold, henceforth all generations will call me blessed;
for he who is mighty has done great things for me,
and holy is his name.
And his mercy is on those who fear him
from generation to generation.
He has shown strength with his arm,
he has scattered the proud in the imagination of their hearts,
he has put down the mighty from their thrones,
and exalted those of low degree;
he has filled the hungry with good things,
and the rich he has sent empty away.
He has helped his servant Israel,
in remembrance of his mercy,
as he spoke to our fathers,
to Abraham and to his posterity forever.'

There's a famous anecdote about the Spanish Carmelite mystic Teresa of Ávila. Travelling in a coach across central Spain, she was caught in a terrible storm. Her coach hit a boulder, and Teresa was thrown ignominiously out of her coach into the mud. Soaked and covered in dirt, she looked up to heaven and exclaimed to God, 'Lord, I thought we were friends, why have you done this to me?' The response came from God, 'Teresa, this is how I treat my friends,' to which her response was, 'If this is how you treat your friends, no wonder you have so few of them!' That was tough talking between friends, not what most people would expect from a renowned mystic.

In some parts of the Christian tradition, the virgin Mary is presented as a model of perfect, unquestioning obedience, the epitome of all that the well-brought up Christian disciple, especially the Christian female disciple, should aim to be. Mary, so the idea goes, embodies in her life acquiescence, humility, self-effacement and perfect serenity in the face of the worst that life could throw at any woman: a mystery pregnancy at the outset of her betrothal; a journey on donkey-back across miserable terrain with the onset of labour as a backdrop; childbirth in a stable as the inglorious ending, followed almost immediately by flight into refugee status in the aftermath of a hideous child massacre; a prophetic prediction that her soul would be pierced with a sword; and a life of obscurity crowned by seeing her son brutally slaughtered. It's quite an eventful career for one who was told that she was so highly favoured by the Lord that the *shekinah* itself, the glory of God, would overshadow her, as it overshadowed Mount Sinai and the people of Israel in the desert. Mary herself might have thrown back that comment of Teresa's: 'If this is how you treat your friends, no wonder you have so few of them.'

Luke's description of the annunciation is itself modelled on the account of God's visitation to Gideon in the book of Judges. Gideon is threshing wheat secretly, in fear of the Midianites, when the angel of God comes in and says, 'The Lord is with you, you mighty warrior!' Gideon is not particularly impressed. Times are hard, and he answers, 'But sir, if the Lord is with us, why then has all this happened to us? And where are all his wonderful deeds that our ancestors recounted to us' (Judges 6:11–15, NRSV). Likewise, Mary does not take Gabriel's message at the annunciation lying down. Being a woman and a pragmatist, she wants to know how the promised pregnancy is going to work: 'How can this be, since I am a virgin?' (Luke 1:34, NRSV).

For Gideon and Mary, as for us, it's difficult to imagine how God's designs can work out in a world where everything seems stacked against us. Mary, like Gideon, has hidden within her a strong warrior, proclaimed by the angel as highly favoured; but also like Gideon, she reminds God that a significant detail seems to have been left out of the equation. It's announced to both of them that God is about to act in power and glory, but Gideon says, and Mary implicitly echoes, 'How can I deliver Israel? My clan is the weakest in Manasseh, and I am the least in my family' (Judges 6:15, NRSV). Both ask for a sign and both are given it. Mary's questions go on. In the few passages of scripture that refer to her, she is generally presented as asking questions or urging God to get moving: 'My child, why have you done this to us?'; 'They have no wine'; 'Do whatever he tells you.'

For Mary, the sign given during her visit to her cousin Elizabeth is one deeply significant to a woman in her position. If God can bring forth life from the empty, shrivelled womb of Elizabeth, God can indeed do anything. The Magnificat, the song that Mary sings on meeting Elizabeth, is no pious canticle. It's a battle-song, a triumph-song of one who exults in seeing how God can and does transform the world and reverse the structures of power. The God of the Magnificat is the one who will confound the wisdom of the wise and the strength of the strong, coming to earth as the ruler born in a stable, the high priest whose rage cleanses the temple, the king whose sovereignty is proclaimed by a notice pinned on his cross, the holy one of Israel who consorts with prostitutes and allows himself to be touched by the unclean.

Small wonder, then, that the Magnificat has become the defining scriptural passage in liberation theology, a theology which emerged from the tortured peoples of Latin America, long oppressed by those who used religion to legitimise the rape of a continent. The account of Mary's visit to Elizabeth is neither simply an historical memorial of the meeting of two surprisingly pregnant women nor a manifesto against injustice, preached at people other than ourselves. The prophet Zephaniah also foretells the manifestation of God's saving power:

Sing aloud, O daughter of Zion;
    shout, O Israel!
Rejoice and exult with all your heart,
    O daughter of Jerusalem!
The Lord has taken away the judgments against you,
    he has cast out your enemies.
The King of Israel, the Lord, is in your midst;
    you shall fear evil no more.
On that day it shall be said to Jerusalem:
'Do not fear, O Zion;
    let not your hands grow weak.
The Lord your God is in your midst,
    a warrior who gives victory;
he will rejoice over you with gladness,
    he will renew you in his love;
he will exult over you with loud singing
    as on a day of festival.
I will remove disaster from you,
    so that you will not bear reproach for it.'

ZEPHANIAH 3:14–18

Here the daughter of Zion represents the whole human race. Our God thrills at the thought of us, lets rip with joy at our liberation and says, 'At that time I will deal with all your oppressors' (Zephaniah 3:19). Like the Magnificat, this offers a powerfully transformative view of God's action in our lives and in our world. But if these readings don't challenge us in our heart of hearts, then they will be useless. We must ask ourselves:

- Who are the princes on their thrones in our own hearts?
- Is there a part of us that is proud of heart, glutted with over-indulgence and sated with wealth?
- Is there something in us that needs to be pulled down to earth, to meet our own poverty and come to terms with it?
- Is there part of us that is so afraid, so wretched in self-denigration and self-rejection that it needs to be exalted by a God who dances at the very thought of us?

Without this first transformation, the transformation of the world cannot happen. Like Gideon, Elizabeth and Mary, we need to clear inner space if God is to act. Without this trust in what God can and will do in us, we are reduced to the mouthing of fruitless pieties. In Mary we don't see a plaster saint. We see a Virgin with Attitude, whose own story calls us strongly to believe that things can be different, that if only we will let it, God's power, working in us and in our world, can do infinitely more than we could ask for or imagine. A poem that reflects this alternative view of the Virgin Mary was written by Anglican priest Penelope Dent and speaks robustly of the liberated Daughter of Zion.

My Fat Virgin Mary

I'm tired of skinny Virgin Marys,
Medieval, milk-mild.
The one I want has a bosom and a heart.
Brooding, maternal and magnificent.
You listen, you love
And you understand.

O most funny,
Glorious, vulgar fat lady.
I love you
And the God who made your
commodious bosom,
Head rest, heart rest
For the uncomforted.

Hold us and love us,
You who dare to be big
And despise corsets.
You who love life
And bottles of stout, pork pies and
bags of greasy chips,
Wrapped in newspaper.

Belligerently beautiful,
Queen of all fat women,
Defender of the unloved.
Accuser of the small-minded, sawdust people,
Who never get involved nor find the
time to love your son,
Wrapped in themselves.

O most funny lady, most funny lady,
Mother of mothers,
Praise be to you for showing us your acceptance,
Your grief and your rejoicing.
Praise be to you for daring to be big,
Proud of your girth
And all Glorious within.

–

REFLECTION

- Look at the questions in bullet points above. What might you say in answer to them?
- Is there anything that prevents you from asking God awkward questions or from believing in God's power to act transformatively in your life and in that of the world?

–

PRAYER

God our creator, only you have the power to change human hearts and to deliver us and our world from all that separates us from you. Help us to believe that you will give us all the grace we need to become transformed transformers wherever you call us to act in your name. Amen.

Walking in the shadows

17 December

Isaiah 40:1–5, 9–11

Comfort, comfort my people,
says your God.
Speak tenderly to Jerusalem,
*   and cry to her*
that her warfare is ended,
*   that her iniquity is pardoned,*
that she has received from the Lord's hand
*   double for all her sins.*
A voice cries:
'In the wilderness prepare the way of the Lord,
*   Make straight in the desert a highway for our God.*
Every valley shall be lifted up,
*   and every mountain and hill be made low;*
the uneven ground shall become level,
*   and the rough places a plain.*
And the glory of the Lord shall be revealed,
*   and all flesh shall see it together,*
*   for the mouth of the Lord has spoken'…*

Get you up to a high mountain,
*   O Zion, herald of good tidings;*
lift up your voice with strength,
*   O Jerusalem, herald of good tidings,*
*   lift it up, fear not;*
say to the cities of Judah,
*   'Behold your God!'*

Behold, the Lord God comes with might,
    and his arm rules for him;
behold, his reward is with him,
    and his recompense before him.
He will feed his flock like a shepherd,
    he will gather the lambs in his arms,
he will carry them in his bosom,
    and gently lead those that are with young.

Nuns are notorious for never throwing anything away, just in case, so whenever they move house there is usually a huge amount of clearing out to do. One of my tasks, the last time I moved, was to downsize our theology library – we certainly couldn't take all those dusty tomes with us – so I had to decide which books were going to be culled. As I got on with the task, I was staggered by the sheer volume that has been written about God. There are books about finding God, losing God, looking for God – but there's no book that has ever been written that adequately explains God, who is always beyond our understanding.

There's a story told of St Augustine of Hippo. He was trying to write his great book on the Trinity, and walking along the beach one day, he saw a little boy busily pouring water from the sea into a hole he had dug in the sand. 'What are you doing?', he asked. 'I'm trying to pour the ocean into this hole,' said the boy. 'But you can't possibly do that,' exclaimed Augustine; 'the ocean's too big to fit into that hole.' 'So is God too big to fit into your explanations,' retorted the boy, and vanished, for it was a vision Augustine was seeing.

Sometimes we may be tempted to think that it's God who isn't enough for us. We can't live on love and praise, after all – we have livings to earn, mortgages to pay, mouths to feed, a future to secure. But as Jesus told Satan when he was tempted in the desert, there's also a hunger of the spirit, a curiosity that wants to know and understand what we're made for and why we're here (Matthew 4:4). It's a passion of the spirit that seeks answers to the unanswerable questions about human suffering, the mystery of love and the great adventure of advancing scientific knowledge, which brings with it as many questions as answers. Isaiah's prophecy is a well-known part of Handel's *Messiah* oratorio, and a passage of scripture used in all four gospels in connection with John the Baptist, who prepared the way for Jesus as the promised Messiah.

Isaiah 40 marks the beginning of what is known as 'Second Isaiah' (Isaiah 40—55), a section which is often called the Book of Consolation. It shifts in tone from the warnings and judgements of earlier chapters to messages of hope and restoration. It's believed to have been written around the time of the end of the Babylonian exile in the sixth century BC. In 587BC, the Babylonians under King Nebuchadnezzar II destroyed Jerusalem and Solomon's temple, exiling many Israelites to Babylon. For about 50 years, the Jewish people lived in exile, unable to worship in their own land.

In 539BC, Cyrus the Great of Persia conquered Babylon, bringing their empire to an end. Unlike the Babylonians, Cyrus had a policy of religious tolerance, allowing conquered peoples to return to their homelands and worship their own gods. In 538BC, he issued a decree (recorded in Ezra 1:1–4) allowing the Jews to return to Jerusalem and rebuild the temple. Such an unprecedented act of kindness from a foreign ruler made him a liberator in Jewish history. Isaiah refers to Cyrus as God's 'anointed', the only non-Israelite given this title. He says that Cyrus has been chosen to fulfil God's plan, even though Cyrus does not know him.

Many Jews did return to Jerusalem and the second temple was eventually completed in 516BC. Some Jews saw Cyrus as foreshadowing the future messianic deliverer. Despite his being a non-believer, they understood him to have fulfilled God's promise to restore his people by ending their suffering and exile, thus enabling the rebuilding of their identity as a people. Isaiah 40 marks the transition from judgement to hope and is a foundation for key New Testament themes, including John the Baptist's role and the coming of Jesus.

There's a hint of ambivalence in Isaiah, nevertheless. Chapter 40 begins beautifully with an image of God as comforting the people through the one who is sent to speak tenderly to them, but even this message of comfort and hope also refers to God as one at whose hand Jerusalem has received 'double for all her sins' (v. 2). Many of the books in the library that I sorted were about the mystery of suffering. There's no book I've ever read which offers a satisfactory answer to the problem of evil, though many great authors and theologians have tried. The best book I ever read on this topic suggests that in general religious people hold one of two approaches to suffering.[13] The author calls these the support context and the meaning context. The meaning context presumes that God directly causes suffering for a specific reason. We expect God to take our suffering away and if this doesn't happen, we at least pray that God will reveal the reason for sending it, so that we can suffer with a sense of meaning. There are many people who can't believe in God precisely because of these attempts to see God as the direct cause of suffering or to project on to God some reason for it.

In the support context, people are not asking 'Why, O God?', but 'Help me, God.' The assumption is that God gives strength for us to live, and strength in suffering. Here faith is grounded in an experienced relationship with God as God-with-us, Emmanuel, made visible in Christ who hangs on the cross with us. Human suffering is an inescapable reality. The ability to experience union with the suffering Christ doesn't give his followers a free ticket to avoid suffering or to find it significantly easier than anyone else. But it helps us to perceive what is potentially faith-threatening as faith-integrating. Our suffering is integrated within our faith not by insights into God's reasons, which remain mysterious and unknown, but by the assurance of God's comfort. The scandal of the cross becomes the strength and wisdom of the faith-filled person.

No rational argument can provide a satisfactory answer to the problem of evil which racks our world. The insights of scripture point to God as unknowable but also to God at work in us through the grace of the Spirit, giving the power for our inner self to grow strong. Isaiah's prophecy here ends with an image of the Lord as shepherd. It's an image repeated in Psalm 23, which reminds us that even if we walk in the shadow of the valley of death, we need fear no evil, because God walks with us.

–

REFLECTION

- Re-read and reflect on the support context and the meaning context of suffering outlined above. Which helps you to make best sense of suffering?
- If you haven't come across the idea of the meaning context before, how might it inspire you to talk to God about suffering?

–

PRAYER

Jesus, you are the loving shepherd of Israel foretold by the prophets and sung of in the Psalms. Walk with us in all the dark valleys of our lives and be our ever-present source of consolation. We ask this in your name. Amen.

What's in a name?

18 December

Matthew 1:18–25

Now the birth of Jesus Christ took place in this way. When his mother Mary had been betrothed to Joseph, before they came together she was found to be with child of the Holy Spirit; and her husband Joseph, being a just man and unwilling to put her to shame, resolved to divorce her quietly. But as he considered this, behold, an angel of the Lord appeared to him in a dream, saying, 'Joseph, son of David, do not fear to take Mary your wife, for that which is conceived in her is of the Holy Spirit; she will bear a son, and you shall call his name Jesus, for he will save his people from their sins.' All this took place to fulfil what the Lord had spoken by the prophet: 'Behold, a virgin shall conceive and bear a son, and his name shall be called Emman'u-el' (which means, God with us). When Joseph woke from sleep, he did as the angel of the Lord commanded him; he took his wife, but knew her not until she had borne a son; and he called his name Jesus.

Thinking about her love for Romeo, Shakespeare's heroine Juliet asks, 'What's in a name?' Romeo is a member of the Montagues, her own Capulet family's hated enemies, with whom they have had a feud for generations. But, she says, a name is only a label – we can change it if we like, and the person is still the same. Names don't matter. But the fact that people change their names suggests that a name does have a deeper significance than a mere social convention for distinguishing one person from another.

In Britain, while people have a lot of freedom to change their names by deed poll, there are some restrictions on what names can be legally registered. The UK Deed Poll Office and the Passport Office provide strict guidelines on what names are not allowed. You cannot, for instance, change your name to anything that would be deemed to incite crime, terrorism or hatred. This would include changing your name to Adolf Hitler, as it's linked to genocide, war crimes and Nazi ideology and would be considered liable to cause offence to the public or to promote hatred. The UK guidelines also block offensive or obscene names, anything that contains racial slurs, swear words, anything deemed inappropriate, and names that could cause confusion, like trying to rename yourself King, Queen, Lord, Duchess, Judge, Dr or similar official titles. Famous names adopted for fraudulent purposes would also be out, so attempts to take a name like Donald Trump or King Charles III would be banned if the intention were to mislead, as would be pretending to be part of the royal family through the adoption of their titles, though having the birth name Charles or Elizabeth Windsor would not be a problem.

The hymn 'How sweet the name of Jesus sounds in a believer's ear' is part of a series called the Olney Hymns, written by John Newton, the famous abolitionist, and his friend the poet William Cowper. Cowper loved the prayer meetings at Olney. In a letter to his friend Joseph Hill in 1783, he described the dedication of the local people, saying, 'I always found assembled forty or fifty poor folk who preferred a glimpse of God's countenance and favour to the comfort of a warm bed.'

I wish I could honestly say that I always find it easy to leave the comfort of my warm bed to pray early in the morning! But the hymn reminds us of the long tradition in the Bible of a name being a source of power, thought in some sense to be a manifestation of the person or deity named. Invoking God's name was, effectively, to call upon God's power. God is a mystery. This doesn't mean so much that God is a problem which can never be solved, but that the fullness of who and what God is will always be beyond our capacity to grasp.

When Moses encountered God in the burning bush, he asked what God's name was. God didn't answer with a noun, a thing that can be contained and controlled and manipulated. God answered with a verb, a word that is about doing, living and being. God said, 'I am who I am' (Exodus 3:14). This can also be translated as, 'I will be who I will be.' I will be who *I* will be, not who you make me out to be. God is not an idol. God is beyond our imagination, incomparably powerful, and yet also someone with whom we can be at home, intimately familiar and utterly safe, known by name.

The Psalms frequently speak about God's name, emphasising its holiness, power, glory and trustworthiness. Psalm 111:9 describes it as holy and awesome, while Psalm 20:7 takes up the theme of safety: 'Some trust in chariots and some in horses, but we trust in the name of the Lord our God' (ESV). Calling on God's name is seen as bringing help and deliverance – 'I will lift up the cup of salvation and call on the name of the Lord' (Psalm 116:13) – and is the object of praise and source of joy:

> The Lord is king; let the peoples tremble!
>   He sits enthroned upon the cherubim; let the earth quake!
> The Lord is great in Zion;
>   he is exalted over all the peoples.
> Let them praise your great and awesome name.
>   Holy is he!
> PSALM 99:1–3 (NRSV)

God's name is often a focal point in the worship of Israel, symbolising his presence, holiness and majesty: 'O Lord, our Lord, how majestic is thy name in all the earth!' (Psalm 8:1). Calling on God's name acknowledges both his greatness and his invitation to be known by his people. It is closely linked to his saving acts and is an essential part of prayer for deliverance and a way to express trust and dependence on his power to save. God's name also represents his justice and the righteousness with which he judges the world; it's associated with his moral authority and his just actions in the world.

But God's name isn't just for public praise, it's also a source of protection – 'Save me, O God, by thy name, and vindicate me by thy might' (Psalm 54:1) – and personal comfort: 'What shall I render to the Lord for all his bounty to me? I will lift up the cup of salvation and call on the name of the Lord' (Psalm 116:12–13).

Swearing, or 'taking the Lord's name in vain', was seen as a serious violation of God's commandments. On the other hand, for many Christians, calling on the name of Jesus is a way of coming powerfully into his presence. In the Orthodox Christian tradition, the frequent repetition of his name in the Jesus Prayer is prayer itself. But just using the name of 'Christian' for ourselves isn't enough if it's just a casual descriptor or indication of a vague group adherence. The name has to go right through us, like the writing in a stick of rock, and make a difference to the way we think, speak, act and live.

Other words and images describing Jesus can also be powerful. In my childhood I discovered the carol 'Jesus Christ the apple tree', a setting by Elizabeth Poston of an early American text. I remember thinking it odd to talk about a person as a tree and struggling to avoid mental images of the Ents from *The Lord of the Rings*, who were talking, walking tree-like creatures. But it's become one of my favourite carols, not only for its haunting music, but because of the consoling central image of Jesus as a tree, offering shade and rest, fruit and sustenance. In spring when blossom promises fruit in due season or when the fruit on trees grows towards autumn harvest, it can be wonderful to think that through God's grace our life and faith can become fruitful. In winter it can be difficult to believe that the bare branches will ever again produce anything, let alone a rich abundance of fruit.

Mary also wondered how she could possibly become fruitful as the angel was promising. The promise to her is the same as the promise to us, 'The Holy Spirit will come upon you, and the power of the Most High will overshadow you' (Luke 1:35).

–

REFLECTION

- If you aren't familiar with it, look up the practice of the Jesus Prayer, or listen to a hymn, carol or song about the name of Jesus, like 'How sweet the name of Jesus sounds in a believer's ear', 'Jesus Christ the apple tree' or Hillsong's 'What a beautiful name'.
- What comes to your mind and heart as you say or listen to the name of Jesus?

–

PRAYER

Loving Lord, we are called by your name. Help us to be your followers not only in name but in word and deed, so that being called Christian, we can mirror your presence here on earth. Amen.

Amazing grace

19 December

Ephesians 3:7–21

Of this gospel I was made a minister according to the gift of God's grace which was given me by the working of his power. To me, though I am the very least of all the saints, this grace was given, to preach to the Gentiles the unsearchable riches of Christ, and to make all men see what is the plan of the mystery hidden for ages in God who created all things; that through the church the manifold wisdom of God might now be made known to the principalities and powers in the heavenly places. This was according to the eternal purpose which he has realised in Christ Jesus our Lord, in whom we have boldness and confidence of access through our faith in him. So I ask you not to lose heart over what I am suffering for you, which is your glory.

For this reason I bow my knees before the Father, from whom every family in heaven and on earth is named, that according to the riches of his glory he may grant you to be strengthened with might through his Spirit in the inner man, and that Christ may dwell in your hearts through faith; that you, being rooted and grounded in love, may have power to comprehend with all the saints what is the breadth and length and height and depth, and to know the love of Christ which surpasses knowledge, that you may be filled with all the fulness of God.

Now to him who by the power at work within us is able to do far more abundantly than all that we ask or think, to him be glory in the church and in Christ Jesus to all generations, for ever and ever. Amen.

John Newton, who wrote the much-loved hymn 'Amazing grace', made his fortune in the slave trade. He was press-ganged into the navy, and it was during a storm at sea that he began a long process of religious conversion. Newton only ever had two years of formal education in his entire life, but he became a renowned preacher and teacher of the gospel. Above all he is known as the mentor of William Wilberforce, with whom he campaigned for the abolition of slavery. Nowadays considered a hero of the abolitionist movement, Newton was slow to realise with full force the horrors of the trade in which he made his money. He spent 40 years as a Christian, still connected with the slave trade, before writing a pamphlet called 'Thoughts Upon the African Slave Trade'. It was sold out in its first edition, while a copy of the second edition was sent to every MP in the country. The pamphlet became hugely instrumental in waking people up to the cruelty and degradation of the trade in human lives.

Newton died in 1807, nine months after Parliament voted to abolish the slave trade in the British Empire. He was aware of the long delay in acting upon his conscience and, like Paul, thought of himself as 'less than the least of all God's holy people' (v. 8). Towards the end of his life he wrote: 'It will always be a subject of humiliating reflection to me, that I was once an active instrument in a business at which my heart now shudders.'[14]

Charles Wesley was another famous hymn writer whose lyrics express the gratitude and love of a disciple reaching out to Jesus in dark times. There are two stories about the origin of his hymn 'Jesus, lover of my soul'. One is that it was written just after Charles and his brother John had been driven by a violent mob from the place where they had been preaching. Another says that the hymn was written just after a frightened bird, pursued by a hawk, had flown into Wesley's window and crept into the folds of his coat. Though neither story can be verified, both speak of confidence in God's healing power.

When John Newton looked back on his life, he saw himself as unclean, a sinner whose active participation in the slave trade made him unworthy to minister to Christ's gospel. We may also be haunted by the memory of past sins, but God's grace is always greater than fault that we can commit. Conversion isn't always an instant business. In the Acts of the Apostles, we see both Peter and Paul growing and developing into the great leaders that they became through a great deal of trial and error, making mistakes, falling out with each other and learning to accept their own vulnerabilities. Grace needs time to take hold and be processed until it's a natural and integral part of our lives.

In Luke 8:41–48 Jesus says an astonishing thing to the woman whose illness has made her unclean, a social outcast. Instead of saying, 'My power has saved you', he says, 'Your faith has saved you.' This is potentially delicate territory. We can't believe or argue that sickness or disability are somehow the result of our weakness of faith or that God punishes a lack of faith with sickness – nothing in the gospels seriously suggests this. But Jesus acknowledges the mutuality of the relationship that exists between the believer and the one believed in – our faith is not an irrelevance or mere icing on the spiritual cake. God takes our response seriously and our journey of faith, our donkey roads and camel treks, matter in a very real sense both to God and to ourselves.

In Peter Jackson's film trilogy *The Lord of the Rings*, Gimli the dwarf and Legolas the elf are reluctant companions in the Fellowship of the Ring, a group of mixed races who undertake a dangerous and epic quest to destroy a ring which holds evil power. They have an uneasy relationship which mirrors the centuries-long enmity between their respective races. As characters, they could not be more different from one another, yet as the quest progresses, they gradually overcome their initial bristling hostility and come to appreciate each other's courage and prowess in fighting. After arduous months facing dangers together, they become close companions, although Gimli is reluctant to admit how much he has changed. In the final film, *The Return of the King*, as they stand bracing themselves for their last and deadliest battle, the dwarf, who began their relationship by shouting, 'Never trust an elf!', looks up at his companion and grunts, 'Never thought I would die side by side with an elf.' The elf looks down at him and smiles, saying, 'How about side by side with a friend?' At last Gimli allows himself to acknowledge the depth of their friendship and says, 'Aye – I could do that.'

The best way to conquer our enemies is to make them our friends, but this involves generosity and humility. We need to acknowledge that our first hostile assessment may not have been the whole story of the other person, and we need to make room in our hearts for affection and appreciation to grow and to allow ourselves to be befriended and appreciated. It's only in this way of 'being rooted and grounded in love' (v. 17) that we can build a sense of peace and belonging together.

J.R.R. Tolkien, who wrote *The Lord of the Rings*, experienced as a young man the devastation of World War I, in which he lost all his closest friends. Eventually, as a survivor of two world wars, he came to know the essential values of tolerance and understanding. This involved letting go of anger fuelled by resentment and bitterness. It's a challenge which faces all of us, not only in areas of political conflict but in our own homes, in our families and wider relationships both personal and professional. It's tempting to slip into attitudes which scapegoat individuals or groups, developing an 'us and them' mentality. During the course of his brutal and unjust death, Jesus forgave those who were instrumental in condemning him. Even as he hung dying on the cross, he offered pardon to the repentant thief. By his grace we can also grow that largeness of heart which can overcome differences, even when they run deep. Forgiveness is a divine attribute, not a human talent, but the Lord's Prayer teaches us to ask for this grace on a daily basis.

In the Christmas story, we see the main characters growing and changing as they respond to God's invitation to cooperate with the great plan of salvation. This is their faith journey, on whatever road they travel. Zechariah is a venerable priest, an authority within the temple and in his own household, but he has to learn to follow God's plan, not his own idea of how God works. Elizabeth has to overcome her sense of shame and lack of confidence. Joseph has to overcome his understandable scepticism and his fear of social stigma, while Mary has to learn to believe in her own capacity for grace. Together with John

Newton, Charles Wesley, Peter and Paul, they come to understand how God's power 'working in us, can do infinitely more than we can ask or imagine' (v. 20).

-

REFLECTION

* How do you understand God's power at work in you and in the world?
* Is there anything that makes it difficult for you to believe that God truly is at work in your life?
* Dividing your life into decades, can you list any gift or grace that you recognise you have received, even when it seemed most unlikely? Take time to give God thanks for it.

-

PRAYER

Lord Jesus, you wait patiently for us to turn to you, longing to heal and liberate us from all that enslaves us and makes us less than we could be. Give us faith, hope and confidence to turn to you in all our needs and to trust that you will do whatever is needed to help us flourish. Amen.

Finding a home

20 December

John 1:9–14

The true light that enlightens every man was coming into the world. He was in the world, and the world was made through him, yet the world knew him not. He came to his own home, and his own people received him not. But to all who received him, who believed in his name, he gave power to become children of God; who were born, not of blood nor of the will of the flesh nor of the will of man, but of God. And the Word became flesh and dwelt among us, full of grace and truth; we have beheld his glory, glory as of the only Son from the Father.

It's characteristically British to dislike pretension. We don't like people to get too big for their boots, so we have all sorts of expressions for cutting people down to size. Someone puts on airs and graces or adopts a grandiose tone and we say, 'Who's he when he's at home with his boots off?' This is based on the assumption that when someone is at home in that state, they are their unvarnished self, the plain Jane or John, divested of any trappings of grandeur that could disguise their ordinariness. What you see is what there is. 'Being at home', in this sense, means being the real, instead of the public figure that we might otherwise cut when in front of an audience.

The idea of God making a home with us and we making our home in God appears twice in John's gospel: firstly, in our reading from the prologue, where we are told that the Word incarnate came into our world, into his own home, and was not made welcome; and secondly, when at the last supper, Jesus invites his disciples to make their home in him as he makes his in them (John 15:4). When we want to put someone at their ease, we say to them, 'Make yourself at home.' Home in this sense is where we feel relaxed and safe, where we don't have to pretend, because we can trust that this is where we are loved and understood, where we can be ourselves and be accepted for who we are.

But it's a risky business to invite people to make themselves at home. When you're at home you can afford not to be too houseproud. It's all very well for us to do this in our own environment, but doing it in someone else's is another matter entirely. To invite them to make themselves at home is to risk your own peace and quiet, your own preferred way of having things done. It means adapting and making space for the other.

Many of those reading this reflection will have been born to the privilege of having a safe and loving home, parents who welcomed them into the world and gave them the best of everything they could afford. People brought up in the Christian faith will have known from their earliest years about the obligation to care for those less fortunate than themselves, but they may have had little idea of what, practically speaking, the implications of such misfortune might be for a person's life. One of the great and unexpected gifts of my own life came about by my falling in love with the culture and literature of Latin America through my university studies. I was also spellbound by the theology of liberation that came from this exotic and faraway continent. There grew within me an increasing sense of being called by God to go there, not because I had something to offer that continent, but because I increasingly believed that it had something to teach me. I found myself praying to experience what it was to be poor among the poor. Be very careful what you pray for – God may very well answer your prayer in ways that you didn't expect and that carry a certain divine ironic satisfaction.

God's first joke was to send me to the one country in Latin America where I didn't speak the language. Being deprived of a voice is one of the primary aspects of true poverty, and as I listened to the unfamiliar speech and accents of Brazil, I experienced powerfully that deprivation and the vulnerability that goes with it. My luggage had remained behind in Spain, so I landed in the freezing cold of the mountains in the middle of a Brazilian winter with nothing but the cotton T-shirt and skirt that I stood up in. I had to beg even fresh underwear from my hosts and found myself homeless, voiceless and inadequately equipped for the environment in which I was living. It was a radical preparation for working among the homeless street children and the thousands who flocked to the favelas of the city from the countryside where they could not make a sufficient living to survive.

'Make your home in me as I make mine in you.' Those words resonate very differently when you already have a safe home to live in and when you don't. I found myself surrounded by people who made their home in Jesus because they had no other practical alternative. It didn't solve their social or economic problems or save them from the danger, humiliation and sheer human degradation in which they lived on a daily basis. But paradoxically enough it gave them a sense of hope, of dependence on God which was so much more powerful than the dependence on consumer goods, status and the trappings of privilege on which my own world relied. When you think you have everything and that you are in control of your own life, you have little need of hope, of faith or even of the love that is willing to sacrifice itself for another. When you have nothing, you begin to experience every word or act of compassion and solidarity as a divine gift. You begin to understand the true value of everything that gives life and allows for human flourishing.

Jesus' words to his disciples at the last supper about making their home in him, the true vine, are challenging in the extreme (John 15:1–10). He talks of cutting and pruning. Anyone who has ever seen the pruning of a vine will know that it's a brutal business. It can look as if the vine has been stripped entirely bare, and it's difficult to believe that anything fruitful can ever grow from it again. He talks of withering and burning – these aren't comforting images, but they say something about the harshness and emptiness of a life lived on its own terms and without reference to the purpose for which all human beings were created. He promises: 'If you abide in me, and my words abide in you, ask whatever you will, and it shall be done for you' (v. 7). But many of us know from bitter experience that prayer generally does not work like that. What can he possibly mean when he promises us fruitfulness when we ourselves feel sterile and empty?

I would never wish to romanticise poverty. Nothing prepares a person from the pampered first world for the reality of how the majority of the world's population lives. But a life where securities are stripped from us, where we know for the first time the true worth of dependence on God and on one another, the power of human solidarity and above all the power of hope, is a life lived to the full in ways that the self-sufficient can never dream of.

Making ourselves at home in Jesus and allowing him to make his home in us is something that we will never manage as long as we depend on our own strength and rely on our own securities. What Jesus offered his disciples on the night before he died was to take a leap of faith, to take on the same risks as he took when he embraced human life in the stable in Bethlehem and when he embraced human death on the cross. They found it a terrifying prospect and when the moment came, they couldn't face it. But when, in the power of the Spirit after the resurrection, they did face it, they discovered what home truly means.

-

REFLECTION

- Spend some time thinking about when and where you have felt most at home. What does or did that feel like?
- Have you ever felt 'not at home'? Think about the contrast. How does that illustrate for you the idea of being at home with and making your home in God?
- John's prologue speaks about Jesus coming to his own home and his own people not receiving him. Is there any way in which he might not feel received or entirely welcomed in your home?

—

PRAYER

Jesus, our loving Lord, you came to your own home, and your own people did not receive you. Help us always to keep a place for you in our lives and in our hearts. May we always make room for you when you knock at our door in the guise of the poor and the stranger. Give us the power to become children of God. Amen.

God with us   21 December

Luke 2:15-19

When the angels went away from them into heaven, the shepherds said to one another, 'Let us go over to Bethlehem and see this thing that has happened, which the Lord has made known to us.' And they went with haste, and found Mary and Joseph, and the babe lying in a manger. And when they saw it they made known the saying which had been told them concerning this child; and all who heard it wondered at what the shepherds told them. But Mary kept all these things, pondering them in her heart.

As Christmas approaches, Rome becomes the backdrop to what might be called a Battle of the Cribs. Each church, and many public places, houses a yet more elaborate and imaginative crib, complete with flowing streams of water, flying angels and noises from the stable. In St Peter's Square, the winning entries from crib competitions around the country make up a spectacular exhibition within the famous Colonnade. One year I visited it and was entranced by cribs made out of a violin or a baseball bat, gloves and helmet. There was a crib in the driver's cabin from a Metro train, a crib in a fire extinguisher, cribs made of newspaper or pasta or drinking straws. There were cribs in spectacle cases and sardine tins, cribs made into a hat and, most gloriously, a nativity scene made entirely out of a 15 kg block of chocolate.

My mother being French, at home our crib featured an elaborate village scene made of *santons*, the traditional handcrafted figurines that are used to create nativity scenes from the Provence region of southern France. Prior to the French Revolution, large nativity scenes would be set up in churches and public squares, especially in towns like Marseille. During the Revolution, religious displays were outlawed, and the church was no longer allowed to display these scenes in public, so people around Provence began to create smaller, private crèches in their homes with figures made of painted clay. As well as wanting to bring Bethlehem into their home, they wanted to bring a bit of their home into Bethlehem, so the traditional biblical characters are all there, but the crèche also features characters representing the domestic and economic life of the region. In our crib we have baby Jesus, Mary, Joseph, the kings and the shepherds and angels, but making their way towards the stable of Bethlehem, we also have the farmer, the baker, the fisherman with his rod, the miller carrying a sack of flour, the parish priest in his *soutane*, a poacher out with his fowling piece, an idle boy asleep under a hedge, old crones with their walking sticks and buxom young women selling flowers, all representing the life of a Provençal village.

There's a similar tradition around Naples, where the traditional *presepe* characters are joined by modern celebrities: film and pop stars, footballers, politicians, and even members of the British royal family. Some places in Provence today have large public nativity displays where the whole town is depicted, with local scenes of daily life. This is meant to show the community's connection to the birth of Christ, with the daily work of ordinary people woven into the biblical story. The *santons* are not merely decorative; they remind people of their own roles in the divine narrative, highlighting the sacredness of everyday life and inviting them to make their own journey to Bethlehem.

The rich variety of characters represented in the crèche can also symbolise the inclusiveness of the gospel, showing that Christ's birth is a universal event, celebrated by all people, from kings and humble shepherds to merchants and even the local ne'er-do-wells. Our crib signifies that God's presence can be found in the ordinary tasks of life and that all of creation is blessed and loved by God. This perspective is taken to new lengths in the film *Love Actually*, where Emma Thompson's character is taken aback when her daughter proudly announces that she has been given her part in the school nativity play, and it's that of

First Lobster. Her astonished mother says, 'There was more than one lobster present at the birth of Jesus?' Her daughter rolls her eyes – of course there was…

There are no crustaceans in our crib, but before Christmas Day we arrange the figures, with the shepherds already there, gazing in wonder at the baby, while the wise men are at a distance in the room, still on their camel trek. As the twelve days of Christmas progress, the wise men start travelling from windowsill to tabletop, getting nearer to Bethlehem, while eventually the shepherds start to make their way home, back over the furniture. Everyone is either drawing near to the great mystery or going home to think about it, but no one is untouched by what's happening in the stable.

If the wise men and shepherds were amazed as they followed the star of wonder, what must it have felt like for Mary and Joseph? For all those swept up in the amazing events in Bethlehem there was a short time of high drama, but then it was over, and there was just another young couple with a baby, struggling to get used to this new person in their life and to their new role as parents. The sheep were still out on the hills, the guests still had to be made welcome at the inn, and everything went back to normal, except that it never could be the same. The mystery was only just beginning to unfold, and it would take the rest of their lives to understand it all. For the wise men, the mystery was still in the making, yet to be revealed. For all the characters in the Christmas story, and for no one more than Mary and Joseph, there's a sense that the events happened at one point in history but the donkey road continued, and the story had a life within their minds and hearts.

That's how the mysteries of faith work. There may be an actual day when we come to faith or make a commitment to God, but faith is dynamic and active – it grows day by day as we ponder God's word and enter more deeply into what it means for us. But like every living thing it needs nourishing if it isn't to fade and stagnate. From Luke's gospel, we hear how Mary pondered the events of Christmas and tried to grow in understanding.

The story of the birth of Jesus shows that God's entry into human history was not without its problems for those who witnessed it. Mary and Joseph had to go on the run as refugees, the wise men had to make their own escape from Herod, and the arrival of Herod's soldiers with murder in mind would never be forgotten by those who suffered the consequences of his paranoia. The Christmas story confronts us with the best and the worst of humanity. Faith, hope and love are found in unexpected people and places. What's common to everyone is a mind and heart either open or closed to God's presence. As we reflect on the Christmas story, we pray always to be alert to the signs of God being alive and active in our world.

–

REFLECTION

If you were to make your own nativity scene, who would you put into it and why?

Imagine yourself in there – what would it feel like to be part of this scene, witnessing this extraordinary moment in human history?

–

PRAYER

Loving God, the coming of your Son into our world caused wonder and amazement to those who were caught up in it. Help us in these days to treasure your words and ponder them in our heart so that we can grow in faith and be convincing witnesses to Jesus, the Word made flesh. Amen.

WEEK 4

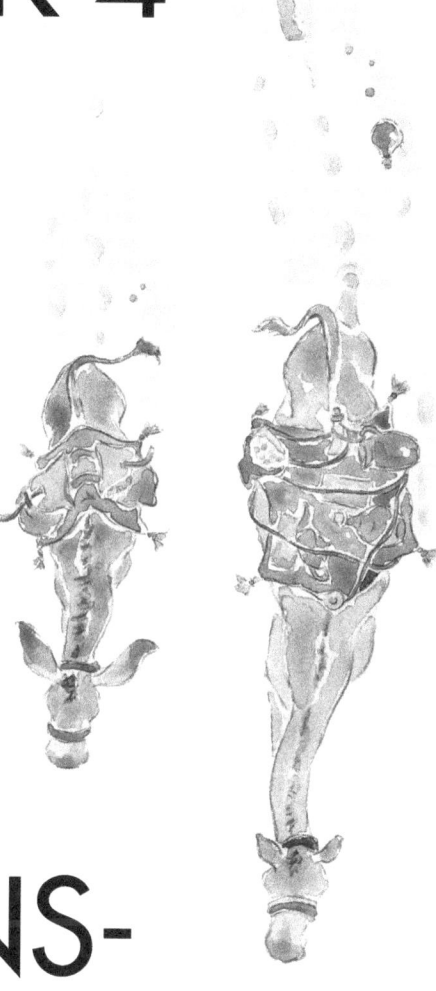

TRANS-
FORMATION

Building the kin-dom

22 December

Philippians 2:1–11 (NRSV)

If, then, there is any comfort in Christ, any consolation from love, any partnership in the Spirit, any tender affection and sympathy, make my joy complete: be of the same mind, having the same love, being in full accord and of one mind. Do nothing from selfish ambition or empty conceit, but in humility regard others as better than yourselves. Let each of you look not to your own interests but to the interests of others. Let the same mind be in you that was in Christ Jesus,

who, though he existed in the form of God,
did not regard equality with God
as something to be grasped,
but emptied himself,
taking the form of a slave,
assuming human likeness.
And being found in appearance as a human,
he humbled himself
and became obedient to the point of death –
even death on a cross.
Therefore God exalted him even more highly
and gave him the name
that is above every other name,
so that at the name given to Jesus
every knee should bend,
in heaven and on earth and under the earth,
and every tongue should confess
that Jesus Christ is Lord,
to the glory of God the Father.

One of the films that seems set to become a Christmas favourite is the animated version of Charlie Mackesy's book, *The Boy, the Mole, the Fox and the Horse*. A beautifully skilled rendering of the 2019 illustrated bestseller, the animation involved more than 120 people from over 20 countries working remotely during the Covid-19 pandemic. The story unfolds as a lost, lonely boy is wandering through the winter landscape. He meets a friendly mole with an unquenchable love of cake. The mole offers to help the boy in his search for the home he has never had. They have various adventures in their search, including an encounter with a fox from whom they hide in a tree, at first perceiving him to be an enemy, but when they find him caught fast in a trap, they try to rescue him. The fox first threatens the mole, but the mole's compassion overcomes his fear, and the rescue is successful. When the mole accidentally falls into a nearby river and is swept away in the current, the fox reappears and comes to the rescue of his rescuer. The mole and boy continue on their journey, the wary fox following at a distance. The group of tentative friends is finally joined by a winged horse, who has been cast out of his herd because of their jealousy at his difference. The rest of the group clamber on to the horse's back to find a home for the boy, but he decides not to go there, having discovered, through his journey, that home is wherever we find love and true friendship, despite all our differences.

At one point the mole asks the boy, 'What do you want to be when you grow up?' He answers, 'Kind.' The root of the word 'kindness' is 'kin', as in kinship. At the heart of Christian conversion is the discovery that, in Christ, we share kinship with God and therefore with all that God creates. We are kin with it all, and therefore we are called to be kind to it all. The first lesson in godly kindness is to learn to see others as equal to ourselves, with equal needs and equal rights. Once we do this, it becomes difficult to ignore them and difficult to tolerate their suffering as if it were less important than our own. It gives us a more balanced perspective on the world in which we no longer see ourselves at the centre of a self-ordered universe, but as a treasured part of an equally treasured community of equals, created, sustained and cherished by the God of all kindness, with whom all creatures are kin.

A number of Christmas carols emphasise the idea of Jesus coming among us to share kinship with us, with all the burdens of humanity. 'Once in royal David's city' has a verse which is not found in most carol books, but which adds to the other, more familiar verse:

We, like Mary, rest confounded
that a stable should display
heaven's Word, the world's creator,
cradled there on Christmas Day,
yet this child, our Lord and brother,
brought us love for one another.

For he is our childhood's pattern:
Day by day like us he grew;
He was little, weak and helpless;
Tears and smiles like us he knew:
And he feeleth for our sadness,
And he shareth in our gladness.'

He is our brother in sharing our limitations and our vulnerabilities, so that, as the letter to the Hebrews says, he can help us when those vulnerabilities threaten to get the better of us:

Therefore he had to be made like his brethren in every respect, so that he might become a merciful and faithful high priest in the service of God, to make expiation for the sins of the people. For because he himself has suffered and been tempted, he is able to help those who are tempted.
HEBREWS 2:17–18

In the letter to the Ephesians, Paul urges the community of new Christians to 'put on the new nature, created after the likeness of God' (Ephesians 4:24). They are encouraged to put off old ways and to think and act in ways consistent with the new person they have become in Christ. He doesn't expect them to be perfect and knows that they will be subject to the same inner struggles that have always been part of the human condition. Rather enchantingly, he suggests that the thieves among them give up stealing. It's an intriguing little insight into the make-up of the early Christian community. He urges kindness because it is one of the characteristics of God and forgiveness because that is the principal gift they received from God in Christ.

The theme of kinship can also be found in the letter to the Philippians, in which Paul urges the community: 'Let the same mind be in you that was in Christ Jesus' (Philippians 2:5, NRSV). Putting on the mind of Christ is a beautiful thought, but perhaps more challenging in its actual practical application. It means putting on the mind of the one who was prepared to enter the home and accept the loving touch and the hospitality of social deplorables, enemies, outcasts and aliens. It means being prepared to:

> Love your enemies, do good, and lend, expecting nothing in return. Your reward will be great, and you will be children of the Most High, for he himself is kind to the ungrateful and the wicked. Be merciful, just as your Father is merciful.
> LUKE 6:35–36 (NRSV)

The kingdom preached by Jesus could as well be called a kin-dom, where we learn to look at one another and see the one who said, 'Just as you did it to one of the least of these brothers and sisters of mine, you did it to me' (Matthew 25:40, NRSV). The beautiful Sanskrit greeting *namaste* can be translated as 'The God in me greets the God in you.' That is the kin-dom which Jesus brought with him when he entered our world. Somewhere halfway up the hill to the Areopagus, the God in Paul, a Cilician Pharisee and Roman citizen turned Christian, found a way to greet the God he had become able to recognise in the pagan Athenians, even if the Athenians did not fully recognise that God themselves. How many of the conflicts in today's world would come to a swift end if that became the norm in the Democratic Republic of Congo, in Israel and Palestine, Myanmar, India, Russia, Ukraine and the United States?

But to give this greeting to others, we must first be able to give it to ourselves. How many of us could look in the mirror and say: 'I greet the God in me'? It is because we so frequently don't understand that God is to be found within ourselves that we fail to detect God in others.

The boy, the mole, the fox and the horse all have their own struggles, but they find a way to overcome them through discovering kinship. I'm not sure that I have grown up yet, but if God were to ask me, 'What do you want to be when you grow up?', I know that my answer would be 'Kind.'

–

REFLECTION

- What issues does the idea of kinship with Christ and the building of a kin-dom raise for you?
- Is there any individual or group with whom you find it difficult to imagine feeling and displaying kinship? What might God be inviting you to do about that?

–

PRAYER

Jesus, our friend and brother, you emptied yourself of glory to become kin with us in all our human limitations. Give us the grace to be merciful to ourselves and, in doing so, to learn to show mercy to all the human family. Amen.

Chosen   23 December

1 Peter 2:4–10 (NRSV)

Come to him, a living stone, though rejected by mortals yet chosen and precious in God's sight, and like living stones, let yourselves be built into a spiritual house, to be a holy priesthood, to offer spiritual sacrifices acceptable to God through Jesus Christ. For it stands in scripture:

> *'See, I am laying in Zion a stone,*
> > *a cornerstone chosen and precious;*
> *and whoever believes in him will not be put to shame.'*

This honour, then, is for you who believe, but for those who do not believe,

> *'The stone that the builders rejected*
> > *has become the very head of the corner',*

and

> *'A stone that makes them stumble*
> > *and a rock that makes them fall.'*

They stumble because they disobey the word, as they were destined to do.

> *But you are a chosen people, a royal priesthood, a holy nation, God's own people, in order that you may proclaim the excellence of him who called you out of darkness into his marvellous light.*

> *Once you were not a people,*
> > *but now you are God's people;*
> *once you had not received mercy,*
> > *but now you have received mercy.*

There can be few things more irritating to receive in our inbox or post than messages and letters which begin: 'Congratulations, you have been chosen out of all the households in Britain to win a million pounds, a new car, a villa in Florida' or whatever it is. The irritation lies in the discrepancy between the promise of the instant prize and the likelihood of achieving it and between the rhetoric of choice and the reality. The rhetoric suggests that someone at head office has been combing the country to find just the right recipient of the company's generosity, and we alone are the one talented and lucky enough to be worthy of the prize, while the reality is that we're in fact one of a cast of thousands whose inbox or letterbox is being filled with yet more junk mail.

All the same, there's something irresistible about being told that we've been chosen – it gives us a sense of our own specialness and self-worth, of having been picked out of the crowd. The supermarket shelves are full of goods proclaiming that the contents have been hand-picked, exclusively selected just for us special people. The letter of Peter also speaks of our having been specially picked by God to be a chosen people, a royal priesthood, a people set apart. Such a passage might make us feel a glow of satisfaction – it's good to feel that one has been picked for the winning team, after all. Or perhaps we feel a sense of unworthiness instead – how could God possibly choose me? God knows what I'm really like; I'm not the holy sort. But Peter isn't talking about the creation of a clerical super-race. He's talking about God's desire for each one of us to be in the world as co-creators, builders of the kingdom, little less than gods ourselves, according to Psalm 8, and this is God's plan for each one of us, without exception.

The Bible is full of stories about God selecting people for a special task, but God's selection procedure is remarkably idiosyncratic. The common denominator in the tales is that none of these people is a likely choice. God decides to create a chosen people and picks as its founders a childless couple in extreme old age. God chooses as spokesman for Israel a man who stammers. When God sends Samuel to anoint one of Jesse's seven sons as king, he is told to ignore the older brothers, handsome, strapping fellows though they are, and instead choose David, a child so insignificant that he has been left out in the fields tending the sheep. God chooses as mother of the Word made flesh not a queen of the orient or a member of Herod's family but a virgin from the poverty and obscurity of Nazareth. Jesus' own choices are no less odd. One could hardly call Peter himself and his fellow disciples the dream team, and several of his female disciples came from highly unlikely backgrounds for the vanguard of a religious movement.

All this is the stuff of fairy tale, showing that God is, indeed, the one person who can make a silk purse out of a sow's ear. The odd choices continue through the history of the Christian church, with the weak, the ugly, the excluded, the repentant sinners and the downright wicked being chosen again and again as God's special instruments. The Christmas story is peopled by a cast of oddities. If we are chosen by God, it's not generally for our beauty or our brains, our strength or our eloquence, though we may find ourselves endowed with these gifts as well. There's some other quality that God seeks in the true servants of the kingdom, and that has to do with openness to grace, to that old-fashioned word 'docility' – a willingness to be led wherever God takes us on a donkey road or a camel trek. Whether it's the shepherds, the wise men or Mary and Joseph themselves, that is at the root of the story of their being led.

God chooses us despite our poverty, or perhaps because of it. But what of our own capacity for making choices? It's a commonplace that we live in an age which is reluctant to make choices, especially those leading to commitment. We have only to look at the falling numbers of people willing to enter into marriage or the priesthood or religious life to realise that a life commitment is a terrifying thought to most of our contemporaries. The world of work reinforces this with a culture of zero-hours contracts, hire and fire, of the need to be multitasking if one is to survive the shift every few years from one company to another. But God doesn't hire and fire. The Old Testament word for God's love is *hesed*, faithful love, the love that clings to us, and continues to hold even when we do our best to shake it off. It's a love that survives all our betrayals, our hesitations and backslidings. The Roman Catholic liturgy of baptism says to every person baptised:

> God the Father of our Lord Jesus Christ has freed you from sin, given you a new birth by water and the Holy Spirit and welcomed

you into his holy people. He now anoints you with the chrism of salvation. As Christ was anointed Priest, Prophet, and King, so may you live always as a member of his body, sharing everlasting life.[15]

The word for priest in classical Rome was *pontifex*, which means bridge-builder – a task that each of us can undertake in all our daily relationships. A prophet announces in word and deed the presence of God in the world. All of us are called to live the values of God's kingdom. God's 'special offer' is to give us the grace to make this invitation a reality in our lives. It's a far cry from junk mail!

–

REFLECTION

- Spend some time thinking of the words of the ritual of baptism. How do you feel they refer to you?
- Within your own life and life choices, how do the threefold gifts of prophecy, priesthood and kingship manifest themselves?

–

PRAYER

Loving God, as we await the coming of your Son Jesus into the world, give us the grace to believe in your call to us to be his living word wherever we are. Strengthen us in faith, hope and love, and build us into your holy temple. Amen.

God's gift 24 December

John 4:7–15 (NRSV)

A Samaritan woman came to draw water, and Jesus said to her, 'Give me a drink'. (His disciples had gone to the city to buy food.) The Samaritan woman said to him, 'How is it that you, a Jew, ask a drink of me, a woman of Samaria?' (Jews do not share things in common with Samaritans.) Jesus answered her, 'If you knew the gift of God, and who it is that is saying to you, "Give me a drink", you would have asked him, and he would have given you living water.' The woman said to him, 'Sir, you have no bucket, and the well is deep. Where do you get that living water? Are you greater than our ancestor Jacob, who gave us the well, and with his sons and his flocks drank from it?' Jesus said to her, 'Everyone who drinks of this water will be thirsty again, but those who drink of the water that I will give them will never be thirsty. The water that I will give will become in them a spring of water gushing up to eternal life.' The woman said to him, 'Sir, give me this water, so that I may never be thirsty or have to keep coming here to draw water.'

God's Gift was a late-night British TV game show that aired on ITV in the 1990s. It was a flirty dating-style competition whose title played on the idea that its male contestants thought that they were 'God's gift' to women. They would try to impress a live studio audience made up of women by performing challenges, talent displays and stunts. The women would then vote for whoever they found most attractive or entertaining, and the winner would get to have a date with one of them.

We tend to use the title phrase as an insult, implying that the person in question is arrogant, self-important and too pleased with themselves by half, yet the opposite is often true. It is precisely because we don't believe that we are God's gift to the world that we are unable to respond to the grace God has lavished on each one of us. This is the point of Jesus' comment to the woman of Samaria about knowing God's gift – she needed to know both the gift and the giver. Her coming to the well at midday on her own suggests that she was trying to avoid the normal time, early in the day, when the other village women would also come with their buckets. Perhaps something about her marital status was a cause of shame and avoidance. This was unlikely to have done much for the woman's self-esteem. Jesus overrides both that cause and the fact that Jews and Samaritans were not on speaking terms and meets her where her deepest needs and questions are.

In today's image-conscious world, there is a lot of pressure to succeed – other people put it on us and we put it on ourselves. On the surface it might seem that we live in a climate of arrogance and self-advertisement. But the truth is that inside, many people find it impossible to value themselves, to find self-worth not through what they have or achieve but simply through who they are, a human being, precious and treasured in God's eyes – God's gift, indeed, to the world. The letter to the Ephesians talks of God's power which is at work in us, doing infinitely more than we could ask or imagine (Ephesians 3:20–21). Perhaps it's a failure of the imagination that prevents us from responding to God's grace. The wrapping of the gift seems so shabby, or so tawdry that we can't imagine that it could possibly hold anything of true worth inside.

The prophet Micah challenges the assumption that we have to earn God's approval or that God's grace can be bought with sacrifice or with effort. We cannot earn God's love like Brownie points, by being good or by toeing the party line.

> 'With what shall I come before the Lord,
>   and bow myself before God on high?
> Shall I come before him with burnt offerings,
>   with calves a year old?
> Will the Lord be pleased with thousands of rams,
>   with ten thousands of rivers of oil?

Shall I give my firstborn for my transgression,
the fruit of my body for the sin of my soul?'
He has told you, O mortal, what is good,
and what does the Lord require of you
but to do justice and to love kindness
and to walk humbly with your God?

MICAH 6:6–8 (NRSV)

Micah was a prophet during the late eighth century BCE, when the leaders, priests and wealthy elites of Judah were exploiting the poor through unjust and corrupt economic practices (Micah 2:1–2; 3:9–11). At the same time, they continued with empty religious rituals, believing that their sacrifices would keep God on their side. The reference to offering a firstborn child reflects the child sacrifice that was sometimes found in the ancient Near East, including among Israel's neighbours, like the Phoenicians and Canaanites. They had recourse to such drastic measures in times of crisis to seek favour from gods like Molech (2 Kings 23:10). Child sacrifice was even found at times within Israel itself, led by kings like Ahaz and Manasseh (2 Kings 16:3; 21:6), despite it being explicitly forbidden in the Jewish law (Leviticus 18:21). The prophets Jeremiah and Ezekiel repeatedly denounced child sacrifice in Israel and Judah (Jeremiah 19:5–6; Ezekiel 16:20–21), and while the worrying story of Abraham and Isaac in Genesis 22 shows God testing Abraham's faith by asking him to sacrifice his son, God ultimately stops him, showing that he does not desire human sacrifice.

Micah deliberately uses the most exaggerated images he can find to denounce the kind of transactional religion that thinks that God's favour can be won with our rituals. The people assume that giving bigger and more extreme sacrifices (thousands of rams, rivers of oil, even their own children) will satisfy God, but Micah insists that God does not want such offerings, but instead desires us to live ethically, practising the virtues of justice, mercy and humility. The God of Israel is not Molech, nor some cruel avenger who delights in humiliating us or making impossible demands. God asks only what we in fact need to be happy: tender love, just actions and a relationship where, like

Adam and Eve, we can take walks together with God in our particular garden. To walk thus with God is both a sign of unimaginable equality and a sign of deep humility. If we can't earn or deserve God's love, then we can't manipulate it. There's something terrifyingly uncontrollable about undeserved love, which is why many of us flee from it. It's better to keep God at a safe distance than to risk receiving the gift of grace with open arms – who knows where that might lead?

There's another facet to this question of Christmas gifts. In the tale of the Magi, we see God not as the all-powerful giver but as the vulnerable receiver. In popular legend the Magi have become symbols of the power of kingship, wisdom and wealth. But this power is worthless if the giver of the gift is not acknowledged. The wise bow down before the simple, giving their gifts to God in order to receive them back at his hands. This is what St Ignatius of Loyola is referring to in his prayer known as the 'Suscipe' at the end of his Spiritual Exercises:

> Take, Lord, and receive all my liberty, my memory, my understanding, and my entire will, All I have and call my own. You have given all to me. To you, Lord, I return it. Everything is yours; do with it what you will. Give me only your love and your grace, that is enough for me.[16]

In T.S. Eliot's poem 'The Journey of the Magi', the travellers go on their camel trek, journeying at great cost to themselves and finding both birth and death – the death of self-sufficiency and security, the birth of reliance on God alone.

The gold, frankincense and myrrh of the Magi are traditionally interpreted as kingship, priesthood and suffering. We all have the capacity, if not the opportunity, to be powerful and wise. We also have a capacity to be holy, and our capacity for suffering is an integral part of that. But wisdom, power and even holiness are gifts we receive from God in order to return them. God is the only giver of gifts who is not insulted when we return the gift. But we return them by using them for God's kingdom, for the furtherance of God's reign on earth.

–

REFLECTION

- The next time you look in a mirror, try saying to yourself: 'I am God's gift to the world.' What thoughts and prayers come to your mind by doing so?
- What are the particular gifts that God has given you?

–

PRAYER

Father of all creation, you come to us wherever we are, bringing with you all the grace we need to live a life of holiness and true meaning. In this Advent season, help us to do justice and to love kindness and to walk humbly with you, our God. Amen.

A sign of contradiction

Christmas Day

Luke 2:27–35 (NRSV)

Guided by the Spirit, Simeon came into the temple, and when the parents brought in the child Jesus to do for him what was customary under the law, Simeon took him in his arms and praised God, saying,

'Master, now you are dismissing your servant in peace,
according to your word,
for my eyes have seen your salvation,
which you have prepared in the presence of all peoples,
a light for revelation to the gentiles
and for glory to your people Israel.'

And the child's father and mother were amazed at what was being said about him. Then Simeon blessed them and said to his mother Mary, 'This child is destined for the falling and the rising of many in Israel and to be a sign that will be opposed so that the inner thoughts of many will be revealed – and a sword will pierce your own soul, too.'

Today is Christmas Day – the day towards which this donkey road and camel trek have been leading. In the commercial world it's often the end of the Christmas season, with Christmas decorations coming down within 24 hours of the Big Day and Easter eggs appearing in the shops before New Year's Eve. But for believers it's the first of a 40-day season which ends on 2 February, celebrated by many Christian communities as the Feast of Candlemas. In between there is the Feast of the Epiphany, on 6 January, which some Eastern churches celebrate as Christmas, and the commemoration of other key figures in the history of the Christian faith – such as Stephen, the first martyr, John, the beloved disciple, and Paul, the converted persecutor – and key moments, like the baptism of Jesus. All of these are closely connected with the birth and ministry of Jesus himself and with Luke's story of Jesus being presented in the temple.

Luke tells us that Jesus, as the supposed firstborn son of Mary and Joseph, was to be presented to the Lord, the first fruit of their union. Mary herself was required by Mosaic law to be purified after giving birth. The infancy narratives of both Matthew and Luke are so full of rich symbolism and multiple significance that it can be difficult to disentangle all the threads, but this is above all a story about how God chooses to enter a particular part of human history, the story of the Jews as the chosen people, and how that choice then extends to all the human race, so that Jesus is acknowledged as the 'light for revelation to the gentiles and for glory to your people Israel'. Subsequent Christian reflection on Jesus' entry into the world as the Word of God made flesh stresses how in him, God makes clear his desire to enter into relationship with us, and how we are invited to make a response to that desire in our turn.

The temple was where God was believed to dwell on earth. And it's here that Jesus is brought in a formal ceremony to be dedicated to God. As often happens, the Christian reader has an ironic overview of the whole story, a sense of 'little do they know what's really going on here'. The worshippers in the temple see what's in front of their eyes, one more ceremony of presentation and purification, but we see Jesus, the Messiah of Israel and God incarnate, coming into his own place. The prologue of John's gospel says that Jesus came to his own people, and his own did not receive him (John 1:11), and there is certainly no record here of a welcoming committee of chief priests and scribes decked in their finery, waiting to receive him. As in the stories of Jesus' birth in the stable, it's those on the margins of history who catch some glimpse of the story's true significance.

From the very beginning, Jesus immerses himself fully in Mosaic law, with all its obligations. At his baptism in the Jordan, he is symbolically cleansed from sin, though he is the sinless one. At his presentation, he is offered to God, though he is one with the eternal Father. This isn't some elaborate charade that he pantomimes for our benefit; it's above all a sign of his total solidarity with our human condition. Where you and I are, there he is. He is fully immersed in humanity in order to transform it. Even the aspects of our condition that seem most God-forsaken are places where he chooses to pitch his tent alongside us.

All the players in this little drama are presented as sufferers of misfortune. Mary has given birth in the most trying of circumstances. She is the only adult character in the Lucan narrative of Jesus' birth who is carried forward into the account of his adult life and ministry, where she appears as the archetypal disciple, who hears the word of God and keeps it. As such, Simeon warns her, she will share in her son's sufferings, as Jesus himself warns James and John that they will:

> 'You do not know what you are asking. Are you able to drink the cup that I am about to drink?' They said to him, 'We are able.' He said to them, 'You will indeed drink my cup.'
> MATTHEW 20:22–23 (NRSV)

Joseph's first ten months of marriage could hardly be seen in terms of conventional bridegroom bliss, either. The portrait of Simeon suggests a member of the Sadducee class, which had largely abandoned its sacred obligations for the sake of political and economic advantage. A faithful Sadducee would have witnessed this betrayal with great pain. No wonder he looked forward to the consolation of Israel. Under Jewish law it was a terrible misfortune for a woman to be unmarried or a widow, and Anna had 84 years alone against seven of married life – not the best of bargains.

Poverty, uncertainty, abandonment, betrayal, death – these are the things that most of us fear most deeply. But it's precisely into this context that Jesus chooses to come. And he comes, we are told, as a sign of contradiction. During World War II, it was widely believed that the Nazis were about to invade Britain. One of the most interesting defence tactics adopted was to remove signs from railway stations telling you where you had arrived, and to change round the arms of signposts in country districts. Everyone local knew that Steeple Bumpstead lay this way and Helions Bumpstead that way, but removing signposts would fox the invaders when they came. Jesus comes to earth as God made visible, God at one with us, but the signs are all wrong, the expectations are reversed, and so the sign goes unrecognised or rejected. But this isn't God playing an oafish prank or trying to fool us. It's the way God is, the God of surprises, not the God of our constructing. The invitation, as the shepherds say to one another, is to 'go now to Bethlehem and see this thing that has taken place, which the Lord has made known' (Luke 2:15, NRSV).

The Christmas story as told throughout Advent is full of people on journeys of one sort or another. This mirrors the lifelong process of conversion which is the journey of faith – it's not for nothing that early Christians described their life of faith as The Way. Whether we are old stagers when it comes to this pilgrim road or just starting out on it, our prayer must always be to have the courage to take the first step, and then another and another, and never to hang up our boots while God still calls us. Christian tradition has Mary as a teenager when she started out from Nazareth and Simeon and Anna at the end of their lives – the call is the same.

The philosopher Boethius (c. AD480–524) was in the prime of his life and at the height of fame and success when he fell out of favour and found himself in prison awaiting execution. As he waited, he wrote *The Consolation of Philosophy*, in which he prayed:

> *O Father, give the spirit power to climb*
> *To the fountain of all light, and be purified.*
> *Break through the mists of earth, the weight of the clod,*
> *Shine forth in splendour, Thou that art fair weather,*
> *And quiet resting place for faithful souls.*
> *To see Thee is the end and the beginning,*
> *Thou carriest us, and Thou dost go before,*
> *Thou art the journey, and the journey's end.*[17]

One of the great biblical scholars, Raymond Brown, who wrote about the gospel infancy narratives, observed that, for some Christians:

> the popular character of these narratives with exotic Magi, a birth star, angelic messengers, etc., means that we have here legends unworthy to be a vehicle of the pure Gospel message. In their opinion this folklore devoid of real theology is fit only for romantics or the naïve… This does no justice to the fact that people who know little of Jesus, beyond his death on the cross and his resurrection, are often acquainted with the Christmas story, which accordingly offers a channel through which the gospel can be made intelligible to them… The infancy narratives are worthy vehicles of the Gospel message; indeed, each is the essential Gospel story in miniature.[18]

I agree wholeheartedly. Many people take their Christmas decorations down after Twelfth Night, the Feast of the Epiphany, but 40 days is an important period in biblical reckoning and gives us time to make the Christmas journey with sufficient time to ponder as we head towards Bethlehem and beyond. The Feast of Christmas is such a wondrous time, so rich in meaning, and the Christmas story so much a whole gospel in miniature that I recommend stretching it out as long as you possibly can. Keep your crib up, your lights bright, your candles burning and your carols being sung until 2 February – enjoy unwrapping God's Christmas present to you every day as you reflect on the Word of God made flesh, God-with-us – and savour every moment!

–

REFLECTION

- Think about the story of Christmas as a whole. Which part of it speaks to you most powerfully and why?
- Spend some time with the Christmas story, with whatever music or visual image you most find helpful, opening your mind and heart to what God is saying to you through this part of the story and how God is calling you to greater faith, hope and love as a response to it. Repeat for 40 days…

–

PRAYER

Pour forth, we beseech you, O Lord, your grace into our hearts: that we, to whom the incarnation of Christ your Son was made known by the message of an angel, may by his passion and cross be brought to the glory of his resurrection. Through the same Christ our Lord. Amen.

Suggestions for group study

The people we see travelling to Bethlehem in the scriptures do it in company. You may also choose to do your Advent and Christmas preparation as part of a group, so here are some suggestions.

Any of the reflection questions given above can provide the basis of group reflection, but some of the questions are more suited to personal prayer. If your group chooses a facilitator, that person can adapt any of the reflection questions or those offered here to the needs and context of your particular group, or use the prayers from one section to go with another reading. The important thing is to use the material in whatever way feels helpful.

For convenience I have offered prayers for the four weeks of Advent, but the length of Advent shifts from year to year, so feel free to organise your 'weeks' in whatever way seems best to your group.

WEEK 1

The overall theme of the first week is journeying from captivity to reconciliation.

1 Do you recognise ways in which human beings are 'captive' as individuals or as society in general?

2 What experience have you had of being liberated from habits, thought patterns or behaviours that held you captive?

3 What do you understand by reconciliation? Which of the twelve habits of reconciliation attracts or challenges you most, and why?

PRAYER ACTIVITY

Spend some time in a darkened space, reflecting on what feels dark to you in yourself and in the world. Light a candle or turn on a small lamp and spend time allowing the light of God's love and power to fill you and the room. Pray for people or situations where you most long for God's light to shine. Is there a hymn or song about light that you want to sing?

WEEK 2

The focus of this week is on the transforming power of God's presence in the world in the coming of Jesus. God calls us to become 'revolutionaries of tenderness', and this has an effect not only on our personal relationships but in human relationships across nations and cultures. It also has an impact on how we view and relate to the natural world.

1 How does the natural world speak to you about God present in all creation? Can you remember times when God has been particularly present to you through nature?

2 What do you understand by the idea of the 'revolution of tenderness'? What would need to happen within you for you to become such a revolutionary?

3 How have you experienced forgiveness in your life? What do you see as the challenges involved in forgiveness? How might we as Christian communities help people to seek and find forgiveness?

PRAYER ACTIVITY

Read together the story of Jesus and the adulterous woman in John 8, taking special notice of what he says about casting stones. Either find a stone or make a picture of a stone. This stone represents something in your life that needs to be forgiven, either by you or in you. Spend time thinking about what it represents and, when you feel ready, lay it at the feet of Jesus and listen to what he says in your heart. End with saying the Lord's Prayer.

WEEK 3

The third week encourages us to reflect on how, in Jesus, God brings us hope despite the darkness in our world and the shadow in our lives. He comes as 'God with us', whatever our circumstances.

1 How do you understand hope and what experience of hope have you had in your life?

2 Are there any stories of people you know or have heard of, or within your own life, of people overcoming challenges and difficulties in a way that inspires you with hope?

3 Does God have a special name for you? If you already know it, or could choose one for yourself, what would it be and why? What does this say to you about the way in which you would wish to relate to God?

PRAYER ACTIVITY

Choose some art paper or any large piece of paper and either draw or make a collage of your name or your 'God-name'. Decorate it in whatever way you choose, perhaps with photos of yourself or other images or words that remind you of your own story. Read out loud Isaiah 43:1–4. How do you feel when you hear those words? If you feel you can, share your picture with others in your group and explain it to them.

WEEK 4

The final week of reflections presents us with the people whose lives were transformed by their encounters with Jesus. The invitation is to ponder the difference that he makes in our own lives.

1   How did you first come to faith? What is precious to you about your own faith journey? Can you share something about that with the group?

2   Has anything shifted or changed in your relationship with Jesus over the years since you first came to faith? Why do you think this might be, and how do you experience him in your life now?

3   What do you think God is calling you to at this stage in your life?

PRAYER ACTIVITY

Write out the words from Hosea 14:5–8, but instead of the words 'Israel', 'Ephraim', etc, put in your own name and, if necessary, change the pronouns from he to she. Read the prophecy out to yourself. If doing this in a group, leave space for each member of the group to speak their own name before moving on with the reading. How do you hear the words, as spoken personally to you by God? Share whatever you feel comfortable sharing with the group. End with a prayer for everyone in the group.

Notes

1   Emmanuel Levinas, *Totality and Infinity: An essay on exteriority* (Duquesne University Press, 1969), p. 179.

2   St Augustine, *On Free Choice of the Will (De Libero Arbitrio)*, Book 1, ch. 6.

3   Quoted in John Moses (ed.), *The Art of Thomas Merton: A divine passion in word and vision* (Franciscan Media, 1981).

4   St Augustine, *Homily on the First Letter of John*, 4, 6, 2.

5   Bernard of Clairvaux, 'In Praise of the Virgin Mother', Hom. 4, 8–9: Opera omnia, Edit. Cisterc. 4 [1966], 53–54.

6   Lynn White Jr., 'The historical roots of our ecological crisis', *Science*, vol. 155, no. 3767, 10 March 1967.

7   Pope Francis, '"*Evangelii Gaudium*": Apostolic exhortation on the proclamation of the gospel in today's world', 24 November 2013, para. 24, **vatican.va/content/francesco/en/apost_exhortations/ documents/papa-francesco_esortazione-ap_20131124_evangelii-gaudium.html**

8   Amelia Hart and Jenny Pennington, *Homelessness in England 2024* (Shelter, 2024), **england.shelter.org.uk/professional_resources/ policy_and_research/policy_library/homelessness_in_ england_2024**

9   Pope Francis, '*Evangelii Gaudium*', para. 88.

10   *The Cloud of Unknowing*, edited by James Walsh (Paulist Press, 1981), ch. LXXV.

11   Julian of Norwich, *Showings*, edited by Edmund College and James Walsh (Paulist Press, 1978), ch. 86.

12   Krista Tippett, 'Hope: reimagined' discussion guide for chapter 6 of *Becoming Wise: An inquiry into the mystery and art of living* (Penguin, 2016), **onbeing.org/becoming-wise-the-book**

13   Richard Hauser, *Finding God in Troubled Times: The Holy Spirit and suffering* (Paulist Press, 1995).

14   John Newton, *Thoughts upon the African Slave Trade* (London, 1788), **cowperandnewtonmuseum.org.uk/wp-content/uploads/2020/07/ thoughts-upon-african-slave-trade-john-newton.pdf**, p. 2.

15   1970 Roman Catholic Missal, see **catholicdoors.com/misc/
     riteofbaptism.htm**

16   See **loyolapress.com/catholic-resources/prayer/traditional-
     catholic-prayers/saints-prayers/suscipe-prayer-saint-ignatius-of-
     loyola**

17   Boethius, *The Consolation of Philosophy*, translated by H.R. James
     (The Project Gutenberg eBook, 2004), **gutenberg.org/cache/
     epub/14328/pg14328-images.html**

18   Raymond E. Brown, *The Birth of the Messiah: A commentary on the
     infancy narratives of Matthew and Luke* (Image Books, 1979), p. 7.

Inderjit Bhogal, Joanna Collicutt,
David Gregory, Esther Kuku, Sanjee Perera,
Gemma Simmonds and John Swinton

Loving My Neighbour
A Lenten journey

Edited by Olivia Warburton

BRF Lent Book

Lenten readings and reflections consider how to love in truth, love the vulnerable and the suffering, embrace difference, care for our world, love ourselves, and love to the very end. It's never been more important to understand how much God loves us and how much he wants us to love each other. *Loving My Neighbour* takes us on a journey through the challenging terrain of how we can truly love one another, individually and in our communities. Daily Bible readings and reflections from Ash Wednesday to Easter Day.

Loving My Neighbour
A Lenten journey
Inderjit Bhogal, Joanna Collicutt, David Gregory, Esther Kuku, Sanjee Perera, Gemma Simmonds, John Swinton
978 1 80039 215 1 £9.99

brfonline.org.uk

Isabelle Hamley explores what it meant for God to become flesh and how this enables us to understand what it means to be human. Seeing humanity in a new light. God became flesh at Christmas. But how does God, who created all things, live within the limitations of humanity – limitations that humanity itself often resents and tries to transcend? And what does it truly mean to be human? As contemporary society grapples with questions of identity, justice and medical ethics, *Embracing Humanity* deftly explores how different aspects of being human are both inhabited and transformed in the incarnation.

Embracing Humanity
A journey towards becoming flesh
Isabelle Hamley
978 1 80039 226 7 £9.99

brfonline.org.uk

How can the light of Christ illuminate this present darkness? This book engages with two great Christmas hymns: the Magnificat and Benedictus. It is also rooted in poets, prophets and the theology and devotional writing of the black theologian and mentor to Martin Luther King Jr., Howard Thurman. Using the lectio divina approach to passages drawn from Isaiah and Luke, *An Advent Manifesto* is an invitation to pray and practise that most ancient Advent prayer, 'Come, Lord Jesus, come.'

An Advent Manifesto
Daily readings and reflections from Isaiah and Luke
Martyn Percy
978 1 80039 094 2 £9.99

brfonline.org.uk

Gordon Giles takes a journey through Advent to Christmas and beyond in the company of familiar seasonal and domestic objects and experiences. Focusing on the everyday stuff we typically associate with this time of year, including some things not so festive, he reflects on their spiritual significance, meaning and message in today's world. Beginning with chapters on journeying and travel, the book moves through major Advent themes of expectation, waiting, mortality and hope to the joy of incarnation and salvation.

At Home in Advent
A domestic journey from Advent to Epiphany
Gordon Giles
978 0 85746 980 9 £8.99

brfonline.org.uk

Celebrating Christmas

Embracing joy through art and reflections

Reflections by Amy Boucher Pye • Illustrations by Leo Boucher

Grab a cuppa and sink into a cosy chair as a father-daughter duo leads you into the celebration of Christmas through their art and reflections. Considering not only the story of Mary and Joseph journeying to Bethlehem, where Jesus was born, but also our modern-day expressions of Christmas, they bring light and life to what can be a fraught and exhausting season. A book perfect for giving as a gift or using oneself to foster joy and peace.

Celebrating Christmas
Embracing joy through art and reflections
Amy Boucher Pye and Leo Boucher
978 1 80039 051 5 £9.99

brfonline.org.uk

BRF Ministries

Inspiring people of all ages to grow in Christian faith

BRF Ministries is the
home of Anna Chaplaincy,
Living Faith, Messy Church
and Parenting for Faith

As a charity, our work would not be possible without
fundraising and gifts in wills.
To find out more and to donate,
visit brf.org.uk/give or call +44 (0)1235 462305

Registered with
FUNDRAISING
REGULATOR